The Journey: Staying on the Path

Chris Futrell

The Journey: Staying on the Path is an encouraging book in discovering the truth about what it really means to be a Christian. Chris Futrell takes the stress out of trying to be perfect, yet shows you how to stay on the right path by giving down-to-earth testimony, and biblical principles.

-   Shelly Wilburn - Walking Healed Ministries and author of the Walking Healed books

Often humorous and filled with insight into the "Christian life", Chris's book brings light into an otherwise dimly lit literary genre; the reality of what it means to be a new Christian convert. Read it. Think about it. Discuss it with friends.

- Travis Cook - Author of If You Love Me...The Commands of Jesus from Matthew

FORWARD

Arguing with God is always a losing proposition. You would think after the myriad of Bible stories about people arguing with God and losing, that I would know this. Head knowledge differs greatly from real world application however. When God told me to write a book, I hopped right on it. I was thrilled to be taking on a task this huge. The idea of being used to help thousands, maybe millions, of people in their relationship with Jesus consumed me. The outline for this entire book materialized in less than an hour. While I never went into a trance or saw visions, I was left no room to doubt God's direct involvement. I started like a sprinter out of the blocks, and motored through the first three chapters in less than a month! Then the fairytale ended.

What I had written so far looked truly inspired, but after chapter three I felt like God had taken His divine help away. The entire project started to appear much larger than it did before. I became overwhelmed. The enemy started whispering to me and I started listening. The Devil hasn't lived this long without being incredibly clever. He started telling me that I was not qualified to write this book. He pointed out my lack of credentials, my lack of seasoning, my shortcomings, and my presumptuousness. Who did I think I was? Who was going to read a Christian book written by a network analyst from southern Illinois? I was in way over my head. The enormity of what I was trying to do, combined with the lack of divine inspiration that I felt, caused me to take a "little break." People in my life who knew I was writing would ask how it was coming, and I came up with a slew of excuses. I claimed writer's block. I explained it as a sabbatical. I even went as far as to claim that God had told me to take some time off.

Months and then years zoomed by and the project started gathering dust. I would pull it up on my PC twice a year or so and write a paragraph or two. I had myself convinced that I was waiting for God to give me the words. Life moved on as it has a habit of doing. This entire project became a nagging afterthought that rarely surfaced anymore, but never failed to make me feel guilty when the thought did appear. People eventually stopped asking about my progress and I felt relieved about that. The less I was reminded about it, the better my disposition remained. It is amazing how easily something, even a directive from God, can be smothered and buried by life. I didn't walk away from God. I didn't quit serving in church. I continued to seek God's guidance and direction in becoming the best husband and father possible. God blessed my family abundantly. On the surface, everything looked great, and for the most part, it was.

Then the arguments began. I had thoroughly convinced myself that I was not qualified to write the book that I had started. I had even begun tossing around the idea of breaking the first three chapters up and submitting them to our church's newsletter. I asked God about this possibility when praying one day and He jumped on me with both feet! He told me in no uncertain terms that I had been directed to write a book, not articles for a newsletter. I argued like a champ, but I got about as far with that as you might expect. For every point I made, God countered with scripture. He brought to my mind the calling of Moses, Gideon, Jeremiah, and Paul. "If I call you to do it," God said, "I will enable you to do it successfully."

Even though many experiences from the "hiatus years," as my wife and I call them, were used in the last three chapters, there is no justification for my lack of writing. I started doubting. I doubted my ability, God's calling, and worst of all I doubted God's ability to use me. God's final argument that finally penetrated my thick skull was this: "My ultimate will is going to be accomplished, but as to whether you will be involved in it is up to you." That got me off the fence. Chapters four through six were completed almost as quickly as the first three.

God can't use stubborn unwilling people, but He also can't (and won't) use someone that insists on doing only those things that is within his or her skill set. If we can do something without reliance on God and His divine enabling, then we are not using faith. It is only when we step out past what we can do, and trust in God to do the work, that we will be supernaturally used. This humbling of ourselves also allows God to receive all of the glory. It is difficult for pride to enter our heart when we are aware of how little we were actually involved. That is the most important lesson I learned throughout the writing of this book.

No, I'm not a pastor. I'm not a traveling evangelist. I don't teach in a seminary. I'm just Chris from Illinois. However, I am a man who was called to do something outside of my comfort zone and then given the ability to complete it. Romans 11:29 in the Amplified Bible reads, "*For the gifts and the calling of God are irrevocable [for He does not withdraw what He has given, nor does He change His mind about those to whom He gives His grace or to whom He sends His call].*" No, I am not a theology scholar, but I AM a child of the King of Kings and the Lord of Lords. That is enough.

The Journey: Staying on the Path

Chris Futrell

Unless otherwise noted, all scripture references are taken from the

New King James Version (NKJV). Thomas Nelson Publishers. 1975

The Journey: Staying on the Path

Table of Contents

Chapter

I really don't want to be that guy

You don't know where I've been

It can't really be that easy…can it?

Yeah, but what about all of the rules

I don't want to be judged

All right, I've accepted Jesus. What now?

I live, therefore I sin... (but I don't live in sin)

Continue from latest save point

I'm telling your Dad!!!

The Red Sea that doesn't part

Why do bad things happen to good people?

I'm a Christian now, why do I still want to sin?

How can a God that is all-loving and all-good send people to Hell?

Why doesn't God answer my prayers?

Is it a sprint or a marathon?

Peter Piper picked a peck of passionate, purposeful, planned preparation

Patience: the universally despised virtue

The greatest trick the devil ever pulled

It ain't in how you start

INTRODUCTION

The following book was written with new believers in mind. That is not to say there isn't plenty in here for mature believers as well. I know that I learned a great deal while reading and studying the scriptures during the writing process. Revelation 2:5 reads, *"Remember therefore from where you have fallen; repent and do the first works, or else I will come to you quickly and remove your lampstand from its place-unless you repent."* The Holy Spirit through John is reminding us that if we forget or neglect the basics of our faith, we can be removed from our place.

The vision that God gave me for this book was to be a resource for new believers; a handbook of sorts, for navigating the new direction recent converts will be heading. People who have little to no experience with Christianity or church are often lost and confused after giving their lives to Christ. I have seen many individuals respond to God's calling and accept Jesus into their heart, only to see them go right back to their former lifestyle the next week. In talking with some of these people, I discovered that they were overwhelmed. They had no clue how to proceed after salvation. Prayer, the Bible, faith, and "church folk" were all major sources of intimidation for these new believers. There didn't seem to be a resource that explained what was expected of them, so they quietly ducked out.

What I felt like God was leading me to do was to create a resource to give new believers somewhere to stand. It certainly isn't exhaustive and it isn't perfect, but it is full of information that I wish I was privy to when I first came to God. I'm sure there are other resources like this on the market written by authors who are much more qualified than me, but this is what God called me to write. I hope to see this publication or others like it used in churches everywhere to provide a foundation for new believers and a reminder of the basics for the rest of us. No matter how far we have traveled in our Christian life, we never want to endanger our good standing with God by letting go of our foundational principles and building blocks that got us to where we are today!

Chapter One

<u>Conversion 101</u>

I really don't want to be "that guy"

I once heard a minister say, "A lot of people don't want to be a Christian because they have family members who are." Wow! Could this be true? Are some believers putting forth a message *that* negative? I am afraid that it is all too true. No doubt, our salvation is God's number one concern for our lives; however, our representation of Christian life to non-believers is almost as important. What many Christians do not understand is that their greatest witnessing tool is not Scripture. First Corinthians 1:18 says, "*For the message of the cross is foolishness to those who are perishing, but to us who are being saved it is the power of God.*" Walking up to non-believers with a Bible and saying, "See here, it says Jesus died for you" is the equivalent of saying to someone, "Hey, I found this book that says food is very bad for your health; so you probably need to cut that out of your life." The very idea that food, a needed component of life, is no longer necessary is completely ridiculous to those whose life experiences tell them otherwise. In the same respect, to tell an unbeliever that the Bible's message of everlasting life through a relationship with Jesus Christ is what they're missing will net very little profit. Our doctrines, rules, and beliefs are not the things that will affect an unbeliever's world perspective. It is rather the example of our life that should draw people to us and increase their desire to have what we have.

Many people, even those who are initially interested in Christianity, are ultimately turned off by the lives they see Christians living. I'm not talking about Christians living like heathens or hypocrites, but by Christians living their lives without compassion, without love, or lacking any form of joy. Multitudes of believers are past "glass half full" or "glass half empty" and are dwelling in the land of "somebody stole my glass." There are far too many people that think, "If being a Christian means being like Aunt Betty, I don't want any part of it." This is a sad testament of the witness that some of us present to the world. We've all seen *Christians* that seem to draw the very sunshine out of the sky. Contrary to popular opinion, a focus on God and doing God's work does not create this type of harsh or even morose personality. Like it or not, that thundercloud stalking the earth is doing precious little to attract others to the kingdom. Unbelievers look at someone like that and say, "Hey, I might not believe in God, but I'm a lot happier than that guy." How can we possibly blame them for thinking that? The truth is, no amount of fervency, focus, or intensity should diminish the absolute joy that comes with serving God. So here comes the beautiful truth: You don't have to be anything like *that guy* to be a Christian. In fact, you'll probably have a much easier time in your walk with God if you steer clear of "Sir Scowlsalot."

The bottom line is that to be Christian is to become more and more like Christ. And just to dispel a few longstanding myths, Jesus was not an intense (grumpy) or preoccupied (disinterested in anything other than His work) man when He lived on this earth. We really need to remove this false distorted image from our mind. Jesus was gentle, caring, and occasionally moved to tears by His compassion for people. He drew people to Him with an unprecedented charisma that exemplified love. I will delve into the subject of the kind of love we are expected to exhibit in a later chapter, but for now, just know that as we become more like Christ we will be more gentle, understanding, caring, and show God's love through our life. Even if you feel like your life is still a train wreck sometimes, you must remember that God has forgiven you and saved you from the consequences of your sin. This alone should put a smile on your face that the world can't take away.

You don't know where I've been

I remember a time that I asked one of my good friends, who had no religious background, to come to church with me. He said, "I better not. The moment I walk through the door, lightning will strike me." What he said was intended to be humorous, but there was a nugget of what he considered truth in that statement. He felt as if God (and everyone in the church) would take one look at him and think, "What in the world does he think he's doing *here*?" I've talked to so many people who simply feel as if they've seen and done far too much to show up at God's house. Contrary to what many Christians think, unbelievers are well aware that they're not living the way they should and don't need or want anyone pointing out the obvious. That is the type of judgmental attitude that keeps them from feeling comfortable around religious people of any kind. Those without Christ in their lives look at us and think, "It must be nice. I'll bet none of them have ever witnessed the kind of garbage I see on a daily basis." Of course this is only natural, since we believers can project an air of absolute perfection most of the time. An outsider would probably think that we came right out of the womb carrying a bible and burping out The Lord's Prayer. In reality, there are many of us that could be an invaluable help to those struggling to start their walk with God, but in our desire to put our past behind us, we have pushed aside our former sinful lives and pretend that they never existed. We have become unrelatable.

If you are one of the millions of people that feel like they are just too far into the red to ever have a relationship with Jesus, I have a couple of life stories I would like to share with you. For the sake of convenience (and my amusement) we'll call these fellows Moe and Larry. Moe was a pretty charismatic guy. He was a beast on the guitar, a heck of a songwriter, a top-notch fighter and an all-around effective leader. Moe did nothing halfway. This guy seemed to have it all, but he had a real weakness for the ladies. His testosterone worked overtime and many times the temptation was almost more than he could bear. He kept his passions under control fairly well for a long time, but the day finally came when he buckled under the weight. And in staying true to his form, he didn't do it halfhearted. He buckled like a true over achiever. He was taking in the view from the penthouse and *accidentally* caught a glimpse of an incredible looking girl taking a bath.

Now I should probably mention that it was a work day, but Moe had been feeling pretty belligerent lately and had been calling in sick for a few weeks straight. He was the boss, he could do that right? In a later chapter, we'll talk about being a good Christian example and showing integrity at the workplace, but needless to say, old Moe was not feeling the whole "work" thing that day. After inquiring about the young lady, he found out that she was married to an employee of his. That should have been the end of it, but he couldn't leave well enough alone. He started an affair with this bathing beauty and even went so far as to arrange for a little accident to happen to her husband so he could move her into his place. Nice guy huh?

Now Larry, he was a religious type. This fellow grew up in church and made it his business to know everything there was to know about scriptures and Godly law. Unfortunately he was extremely arrogant about his knowledge. Larry was so full of himself and so assured in his knowledge, he would travel around looking for people who believed differently and harass them. His overseers even gave him the power to arrest and even torture people of different beliefs. There is even one documented story about Larry acting as the coat check attendant at a public execution. He felt as if he were purging the world of any teaching that might cause his understanding to be questioned. Larry sounds like a real peach, right?

Now I think we all know how the real world would pronounce judgment on these fellows. You reap what you sow, right? If you do the crime, you do the time. If you mess with the bull, you're going to get the horns. [Insert applicable cliché here.] What did happen with these thoroughly disreputable men? You might be surprised. Moe is actually King David, a fellow who the Bible calls "a man after God's own heart." (Acts 13:22) Larry, aka the Apostle Paul, went on to become the greatest missionary in the Bible and wrote over half of the New Testament. How is this possible? The answer to that is simply the mercy and grace of a loving God. Both of these men were living lives of despicable evil, but when God selected them to be His vessels, they accepted that call and became led by Him. God turned their weaknesses into strengths and used both of them to shake the nations.

Now here is the recipe that is one part shocking and two parts awesome. God is not only *able* to turn lives around in this type of jaw-dropping manner, but He delights in it. It makes Him giddy. There is little that pleases God more than to take a factory defective, rusted out, barely drivable death trap and transform it into a "holy hotrod. There is nothing that you could do that would disqualify you for a God-makeover. Not only is He able, but He greatly desires to show off on your behalf. When you come to God and accept His Son into your heart, the blood of Jesus makes you appear perfect before God's throne.

It can't really be that easy...can it?

OK, where's the dotted line I need to sign to begin this journey? What are the terms of my surrender? Where is the list of everything I have to give up? These are pretty common questions for unbelievers that want to turn their life around. They might not use those exact words, but this is how they think about starting a life with God. Kind of sad, isn't it? This head-hanging sense of defeat, surrender, and guilt, that is commonly associated with Christian conversion, is incredibly depressing. Unfortunately, it is we (the seasoned believers) that foster this defeated mentality. We tell these babies in Christ that their life will change (true) and that those changes must be self-imposed (most emphatically--not true). We assure them the way will be hard and they will be miserable for a while; but if they succeed in denying the flesh of every wanton desire through good old fashion willpower, they will attain the position of God's child. I may be overstating things a bit, but not by much. Then we wonder why they stop coming to church after three weeks. I guess they just weren't ready yet.

Let's find out what the Bible says about this birthing process into God's kingdom. Where in God's Word is this contract of gloom and suffering (but life everlasting)? Well, according to the inspired word of God, this tumultuous event is accomplished in two integral steps. The first is located in Acts 26:20 which says, "*but declared first to those in Damascus and in Jerusalem, and throughout all the region of Judea, and then to the Gentiles, that they should repent, turn to God, and do works befitting repentance.*" Asking God to forgive you for your sins and choosing to believe that His grace will change you into a creature that is more characteristic of Jesus is step one. Step number two is declared in Romans 10:9 which says, "*that if you confess with your mouth the Lord Jesus and believe in your heart that God has raised Him from the dead, you will be saved.*" What?? No hoops to jump through? No doctrinal rhetoric to memorize? I'm afraid not. If you ask for it, receive it, and believe it, salvation and eternal life are yours. Sweet deal huh?

Naturally, there are changes that need to be made by you. In Romans 13:14, Paul wrote, "*But put on the Lord Jesus Christ, and make no provision for the flesh, to fulfill its lusts.*" Paul is admonishing the Roman church to do nothing to foster our human nature's worldly appetites. We should always strive to do our best to live like Christ, but those are shoes that we cannot possibly hope to fill on our own. When called upon, our Holy Father is exceedingly glad to help us with His strength. Only by His grace and mercy are we able to aspire to such heights.

Yeah, but what about all of the rules

Ah yes, the "list of don't." Almost all unbelievers and freshly converted Christians seem to think that this list is hiding somewhere in every church. Perhaps it is in the mysterious third drawer of the pastor's desk. Or maybe it is in a secret compartment under the baptismal tank. Wherever it is located, nearly everyone who wants to turn their life over to God is waiting for the moment of truth when they are presented with the legendary "list of don't." There are a few "do's" on the list as well, but this list (as everyone knows) is primarily littered with "don't." Eventually the pastor, or one of his staff members, will call you into a private office and give you the following speech.

"Here is your copy of the "List of Don't". This strict curriculum is put in place for your own good. God knows that your desire to please Him isn't going to be nearly enough to enter the straight and narrow gate.

Therefore, to correct this obvious oversight by the Savior, a comprehensive proclamation of "evil" has been issued by . . . well, it's someone important and super holy, I'm sure.

Let me assure you, this will eliminate all of the pressure of trying to hear from God for yourself. Deciphering the nearly cryptic word of God? No longer an issue. Believe me; it is much easier to be programmed like a computer than to use the brain that God gave you."

While no church or religious organization would ever say anything like this to anyone, this attitude and mentality epitomizes many people's idea of conversion. However, the truth is that this school of thought is counterproductive to Christianity. It produces feeble minded and immature Christians who have no concept of how to release their faith to do battle with the enemy or their human nature. Baby Christians incubated in this robotic style of service to God are constantly feeling weak and ineffective in their spiritual walk. Half of the rules they don't understand, and the other half they submit to unwillingly thinking it is the only way to please God. The beautiful reality is that no one can author your relationship with Jesus but you. Your walk with God is personalized and one of a kind. The whole reason for coming to God is a longing for something more out of life, and no list or set of rules is going to fill that void.

Before the birth of Christ, God operated by rules and edicts. He gave His people a detailed set of laws that had to be followed to the letter. Why? Before Jesus' coming to earth, God did not dwell inside of people's hearts. It was more of a master/servant relationship. Since the only contact with God was through a prophet (or the occasional burning bush), these rules were the only way for the Israelites to show their loyalty and worship to God. However, when God sent his Son to earth to become the ultimate sacrifice for all of mankind's sin, He sent His Spirit, the Holy Spirit, to live inside of us. He changed our relationship with Him from master/servant to father/son. He tells us in Romans 8:6, "*But now we have been delivered from the law, having died to what we were held by, so that we should serve in the newness of the Spirit and not in the oldness of the letter.*" His Spirit now serves as our guide and conscience. The more we mature in Christ, the more the Spirit will guide and direct us in what we need to do and not to do. The more that we seek after God and try to please Him, the more characteristic we will become of His Son. God's Spirit will help to mold you and direct you in the direction to go, but your obedience is the key to stepping into what He has planned for you. We will deal with obedience more extensively in a later chapter.

But I don't want to be judged

For a new Christian, one of the most difficult things to deal with is the perception of being looked down upon or scorned for how they live. The sidelong glances and whispering will cut a new brother or sister to the bone. I would love to tell you that upon your conversion, all fellow believers will accept you in love and show the compassion of a saint as you are growing in God's grace. However, even Christian people deal with that pesky problem of imperfection. Imperfection is the thorn in our side that seems to plague us for our entire life. I've met some people who claim that they have overcome this nasty little pestilence, but I have my doubts. The truth of the matter is that as long as we continue to draw breath, we will not achieve perfection. Many of us truly want what's best for these new converts, but we still tend to put on our powdered wig, grab our gavel, and deliver our scathing (if silent) opinion of what we consider "their sin."

We would be so much better off if we, the experienced Christians, could swap our blinding spotlight for a beacon. We need to be a lighthouse for Christ that draws these new Christians into an ever deeper relationship with God instead of a religious flashlight that points out other's shortcomings. I think that many churches need a large sign above the front door that reads, "Warning: Constantly taking the high road may cause nosebleeds." We may not like to hear this, but we're not qualified to judge anyone. This doesn't mean we condone or approve of sin. It also doesn't mean that we are not allowed to speak correction (with love) into someone's life if God is leading us to do so. However, our primary job is to help these new believers mature and grow until they get revelation from God themselves. God is the one with the right and the righteous ability to act as judge. The concept of sowing and reaping is prevalent throughout the entire Bible, and this spiritual law doesn't take a hiatus when dealing with judging. Mathew 7:1-2 declares, "*Judge not, that you be not judged. For with what judgment you judge, you will be judged: and with the measure you use, it will be measured back to you."* This self-feeding cycle of judging and being judged will result in much hurt and eventually destruction. For now I'll keep it simple and quote Jesus as He said "Let he who is without sin cast the first stone."

I do have a few pieces of advice for the new Christians who have to deal with this judgmental spirit. First of all, remind yourself constantly why you have started this walk with God. This will help you to tune out a lot of the garbage that goes on in the "holier than thou" demographic. Next, you need to find some compassionate mentors and friends in the church that will encourage you in your new faith. To a baby Christian, isolation can be devastating. Especially when also having to deal with judgmental attitudes and spirits from fellow believers. Starting a journey with God is much like parenting your first child. Sometimes pain results from moving someone else onto the top of your priority list. Many new believers have been living for themselves for decades. Just like becoming a parent for the first time, you have to make a conscience choice to make someone, other than you, the focus of your life. You will be busy enough learning how to accomplish this task without having to deal with knuckleheads who feel the need to point and whisper. The only One you need to worry about pleasing is God, and He will guide you in this.

The flip side of this coin is just as dangerous. In my years in and out of church, one of the most prevalent attitudes I see is: "Don't judge me." It is God's job to judge, but it is also God's job to correct people on their judgmental attitude. Don't use God's word as a weapon against people. We are to use the Bible as our guideline against sin in our own lives, not to tell everyone what they're doing wrong. Ninety percent of people who use the phrase "Don't judge me" are looking for acceptance for their sin. God never told us to turn a blind eye to sin or worse yet, embrace it. However, if God desires you to approach someone else about their sins, He will open the door and let you know. Don't take it upon yourself! Let's worry about removing the sin from our own lives before worrying about everyone else.

Chapter 2

<u>CSI: Christ Seeking Individuals</u>

All right, I've accepted Jesus. What now?

Starting your walk with God is a lot like starting a new

relationship... umm...actually, it is nothing like that, but there is one common

thread. When you are really interested in someone, you desire to find out

everything that you can about them. What do they like? What do they find

disgusting? What makes them tick? This goal is normally accomplished by

conversation and communication. We spend hours on the phone, send

thousands of texts and instant messages. Some even participate in the archaic

art of letter writing (assuming that anyone knows how to spell or use a pen

anymore). If you find out that your new love interest's favorite color is

purple, you send violets to her job, or buy him a purple Jaguar XF convertible

(Hey fellas, I'm trying). If you discover he or she is an animal rights activist,

a home rental of "Free Willy VI: Willy, He's in the Army Now" is probably better than a big game hunting safari. The bottom line is that you try to do whatever you can to please your new *friend*.

Your journey with God should begin in much the same way. Your first priority should be getting to know Him and finding out everything you can about what He likes, dislikes, and what generally makes Him tick. There is one huge advantage to a new relationship with God over a new relationship with a person. Very few people you develop an interest in already have a *tell-all* autobiography published and free for the reading. However, this is just what God has provided. His word, the Bible, can tell you just about everything there is to know about Him. What pleases Him, what angers Him, and even what stirs Him to jealousy can all be found in those pages. How convenient, huh? No need for sneaking around and asking His friends for information. No driving compulsively around His block wondering what time He gets off work. No Facebook stalking. Best of all, there will never be any charges brought against you for criminal trespass because God wants you to know everything possible about Him. Deuteronomy 6:5 declares, "*You shall love the Lord your God with all your heart, with all your soul, and with all your strength,*" while Acts 17:26-27 says, "*And He has made from one blood every nation of men to dwell on the face of the earth, and has determined their pre-appointed times and the boundaries of their dwellings, so that they should seek the Lord, in the hope that they might grope for Him and find Him, though He is not far from each one of us.*" You see, God wants us to know and love Him at all costs. By reading and studying His word, and spending time communicating with Him, we can begin to know who He really is. Religion has, at times, put entirely too much focus on knowing *about* Him, but not nearly enough emphasis on *knowing* Him personally. Your personal voyage with God should always reflect your fervent desire for relationship, not religion.

Here is the part where I would love to tell you about the constant state of joy, peace, and victory in which you will be living. Nothing would delight me more that to explain to you the perfect state of contentment that is now yours. It would give me the deepest of pleasures to assure you that there will always be a ham in every refrigerator, a hybrid in every driveway and a fat bonus on every paycheck. As much as I would enjoy telling you these things, sadly, I cannot. Unfortunately, if you're going to buy into Christianity, you have to take the hard with the easy. There are going to be tough times.

Life on earth, by its very nature, has peaks and valleys. Satan is an enemy of our soul and will put forth his best effort to thwart your victory and peace. His attacks will become more vicious as you become more of a threat to him. Your flesh (natural human instinct), which was corrupted by the weakness and fall of the first man and woman, will wage war against your best intentions. However, there is no problem, addiction, sickness, or disaster that is bigger than God. First John 4:4 reads, "*You are of God, little children, and have overcome them, because He who is in you is greater than he who is in the world.*" Not only is He greater, but He desires to help you through any trial as long as you believe that He will. First Corinthians 10:13 declares, "*No temptation has overtaken you except such as is common to man; but God is faithful, who will not allow you to be tempted beyond what you are able, but with the temptation will also make the way of escape, that you may be able to bear it.*" How fantastic is that? God will never allow you to get to the breaking point, and has, in fact, already pre-planned an escape route for you.

All in the family

When I was in my callow youth, I used to tell my mother that I didn't want to go to church because there were way too many hypocrites there. She just smiled and told me not to throw out the baby with the bathwater. As I got older and less rebellious, I started to understand what she meant. There is no such thing as a perfect church, because there is no such thing as a perfect person and churches are made up of people. The contention that you are looking for the perfect church is a cop-out of epic proportion. In studying people, I have discovered that if you are looking for flaws you will find them every time. If you go somewhere and are just waiting to be offended, you won't have to wait long. To put it simply, if you attend a church and the pastor has never stepped on your toes, at least occasionally, then one of you is unnecessary. Either you have it all figured out, or the pastor is swinging and missing. Don't let fear or pride stand in the way of the spiritual growth that you so desperately need to function in today's society. This spiritual growth depends on finding a local house of worship.

Strength, preparation, instruction, and fellowship are all vital reasons for finding a church home. I will tell you right up front that I will not lobby for any particular denomination or organization. Christ did not institute any specific brand or flavor of Christianity. That flies in the face of what many Christians would have you to believe, but the early church was just that, the church. Finding your place to worship and mature in God is deeply personal and somewhat subjective, but I will give you a few pointers. Find a church that believes the Bible is God's authoritative and final word and that will supply an atmosphere where you are spiritually challenged and fed. Find a church that will encourage you to grow and become involved in adding to the kingdom of God.

I've talked to many people who shun the entire idea of organized religion for various reasons and claim to have their own "church time" at home. For years I was one of these people. However, the Bible clearly states God's will for us in Hebrews 10:25. It says, "*not forsaking the assembling of ourselves together, as is the manner of some, but exhorting one another, and so much the more as you see the Day approaching.*" You will often hear people say that it doesn't matter where you go to church as long as you go. The sentiment behind that statement is heartfelt, but it is not exactly true. Whereas I won't point you toward any specific church, God will. He has a place in His will that has a *you-shaped hole* in it. He has a church that needs exactly what you have to offer and He gives you the grace to do that job better than anyone else. If you seek after God and His will, you will end up exactly where He wants you to be.

From the beginning, and I mean the very beginning (Genesis 2:18), God knew that man would need companionship, and He hasn't suddenly changed his mind now. Brothers and sisters in Christ are essential for growth, maturity and especially support. Hebrews 3:13 reads, "*but exhort one another daily, while it is called 'Today', lest any of you be hardened through the deceitfulness of sin.*" A tight knit church family will provide every Christian with multiple wells of knowledge and experiences from which to draw. Everyone goes through tough times and stretches of weakness. However, with caring brothers and sisters, you can be almost certain that there will be someone in your church family who has weathered the same storms and has invaluable lessons on how to persevere. Many Christians find that their individual ministry involves helping others with battles that they have already overcome. God enjoys turning the weaknesses in our nature into strengths for Him.

Aside from it being God's command and the need for a spiritual support system, the other necessity of church comes from your need for a shepherd. During His earthly ministry, Jesus referred to the kingdom of God (later the church) as the flock and Himself as the shepherd. In Ephesians 4:11-12, the apostle Paul writes about the call of God on people's lives saying, "*And He Himself gave some to be apostles, some prophets, some evangelists, and some pastors and teachers, for the equipping of the saints for the work of ministry for the edifying of the body of Christ.*" When God calls someone to the office of pastor, to be overseer of His flock, there is an anointing that goes with that office to feed and nurture the body of Christ (church members). Romans 10:17 reads "*So then faith comes by hearing, and hearing by the word of God.*" Therefore, by sitting under a called and anointed pastor, you are being led into greater faith. And without faith it is impossible to please God (Hebrews 11:6). This type of pastor will always provide you with instruction and tools to do the job that God has called you and every other Christian to perform; the primary job being adding people to His kingdom.

The Bible isn't a storybook

Without a doubt, the Bible contains some of the most incredible and enjoyable stories ever published. From the story of creation, we jump right into "paradise lost" through the agent of a talking snake and the marital blame game ("It was that woman that You gave me") that goes on to this day. After that, we delve right into the first murder and a flood destroying the earth and everyone on it except for one family that found favor with God. We immediately proceed to the descendants of that family and the story of a great tower being built in an attempt to reach the heavens. From there we see the destruction of two major metropolitan cities by the raining down of fire and sulfur. We see a person being supernaturally turned into a pile of dinner seasoning, the first surrogate mother, sibling rivalries, a wrestling match with an angel, and by the way, we're not even halfway through the first book of the Bible. You'll see a talking donkey, a man being partially digested by a huge fish and living to tell about it and a holy infestation of frogs on an entire country.

God's word is truly a collection of the most astounding stories ever heard. That being said, the purpose of the Bible is not to entertain and enthrall us. It was not written to provide a nice tale or two before bed or scare your kids into submission (although there are numerous parents that use God's word for that very purpose). There are many provisions of the Bible, but I believe that they can be condensed into three major precepts.

Communication is the general give and take of information, thoughts, feelings, and opinions. Earlier in this chapter, I discussed the importance of getting to know someone when entering into any kind of relationship with that person. Communication is the primary way of establishing the foundation for a friendship or relationship. Effective communication is also essential for maintaining an open and honest relationship. Lack of communication is the number one culprit in destroyed marriages, failed businesses, and broken family ties. Many issues and problems have a way of being resolved through healthy, candid communication. Our relationship with God is no different. It takes communication on both ends to ensure a stable bond with our Savior. The Bible provides a way for God to communicate with us and is the first major purpose of His word.

One of the most frustrating feelings for any Christian is the occasional sense that our relationship with God is heavily one-sided. We talk to Him, but he very rarely talks back, at least in the conventional sense. This "silence" from our Savior has been sermonized, taught upon, and explained away by many well-meaning Christians and even pastors. However, as is the case in many of these Christianity issues, we have made it much more complex than what it is. The Bible is the chief method used by God to communicate with His saints. I understand the first question on many lips. How can a book that is thousands of years old communicate with us now?

Hebrews 4:12 says, "*For the word of God is living and powerful, and sharper than any two-edged sword, piercing even to the divisions of soul and spirit, and of joints and marrow, and is a discerner of the thoughts and intents of the heart.*" This is no ordinary book we are talking about; this is the God-breathed word of our Lord. According to this passage, the word of God can discern (to see or know something that is not obvious; understand) the thought and intents of our hearts. That's a powerful piece of literature. This makes the idea of a two thousand year old book being a current communication medium a bit more plausible. God wants to talk to you every day, but many of us are looking in the wrong places. Opening up this two-way dialogue with the Master is essential in strengthening your walk with Jesus.

In the Gospel of John, chapter 14:21 Jesus said, "*He who has My commandments and keeps them, it is he who loves Me. And he who loves Me will be loved by My Father, and I will love him and manifest Myself to him.*" To manifest means to make visible or exhibit. So if we have and keep His commandments, He will show Himself to us in a visible way. I don't know about you, but I like the sound of that. For many people, even Christians, God is some celestial body that has no real definition or palpable presence. However, God can be as real to us as the people we see every day and more so. In this scripture, Jesus tells us His desire to reveal Himself to us as we cherish and keep His words and instructions. After all, our ultimate purpose is to try to be more like Christ. How can we know what He was like if we don't spend time reading and studying His word?

Have you ever awakened in the middle of the night and tried to make it through the house in the pitch black? If it is your own house, you might do a pretty decent job at navigating the darkness. However, what if someone had come in and rearranged everything in your house after you had fallen asleep. Would you still be able to make it to the restroom or kitchen in the dark? I would foresee a number of stubbed toes in your immediate future. Navigating our way through life is much like navigating through a strange house in the dark. Our world seemingly changes from one day to the next, and nothing ever seems to stay the same. Many times, we as humans feel like we are groping our way through total darkness. Even nonbelievers are quick to say that we are living in dark times. It is in this pitch black, confused, and turned around state that we discover the second concrete purpose of God's holy word.

Psalms 119:105 reads, "*Your word is a lamp to my feet and a light to my path.*" The majority of people who convert to Christianity are in an extremely dark place. It could be a drug addiction, broken marriage, alcoholism, or just a general weariness of the direction of their life. Needless to say, a light is more valuable to someone in the dark than anything else they could receive. Accepting Jesus will bring some definite light into your life, but the circumstances that you are in are not just going to disappear. You need a light to help lead you out of the darkness. The Bible is God's primary way of giving you that light. His word is full of instruction, encouragement, and tools to help you combat the darkness that has reigned over your life. In addition, the Bible contains the master key for allowing God to become "real" to you in a way that didn't seem possible before.

The third use of the Bible is also the least employed, even by the majority of the church world. The Bible is our weapon. According to state and federal law, I need to clarify that while the 25 pound, leather bound, coffee table centerpiece, King James, Illustrated Bible would make an excellent blunt instrument against home intruders; there are legal ramifications of performing Bible bludgeoning. And far be it from me to discount the nasty infections that can set in from a deep paper cut. However, we need to know that God's word is a spiritual weapon that has the makings of a very bad day for Satan. Our battle with Satan and our sinful nature is played out daily in our lives and minds.

The enemy will use any tactic possible to accomplish the goal of getting you to quit your walk with God. Some of the more common methods he will use include depression, sickness, addiction, poverty, and confusion. What do we have to fight back against this onslaught? Ephesians 6:17 reads,

"*And take the helmet of salvation and the sword of the Spirit, which is the word of God.*" God provided His word to be a weapon against any trial or temptation that you may have to endure. How does it work? Faith that God's word is completely true and confession with our mouth are the two keys.

If His word gives us a promise and we confess it, and believe it with all of our heart, then God will act. It's a spiritual law. God is faithful to His word and responds to our faith in it. Mark 11:22-24 declares, "*So Jesus answered and said to them, 'Have faith in God. For assuredly, I say to you, whoever says to this mountain, 'Be removed and be cast into the sea', and does not doubt in his heart, but believes that those things He says will be done, he will have whatever he says. Therefore I say to you, whatever things you ask when you pray, believe that you receive them, and you will have them.*'" So if sickness is upon us, we quote Isaiah 53:5 and claim that "*by His stripes we are healed.*" If we are strapped financially, we confess Philippians 4:19 and say, "*All of my needs are met according to His riches in glory.*" If we are tempted to sin, we speak I John 4:4 over our lives and say, "*He who is in me is greater than he who is in the world.*" God will never abandon us in our hour of need, and has provided tools to combat the darkness in our lives through His holy word. We'll spend some more time later discussing the use of scriptures and *speaking life* over yourself and your circumstances.

God calls each one of us to be a disciple for Him. The word disciple is obviously based on the word discipline. Discipline is required for any task that is important in our lives, and spending time in His word is no different. There are days that I would rather color-code my dryer lint than study the Bible. That may sound horrible, but anyone who has been a Christian for any length of time can sympathize with that attitude. There are many times that I feel drawn to scripture and feel like I can't make it without a healthy dose of word, but it isn't always like that. Sometimes I have to make myself spend time in reading and studying. Just like dieting, exercise, or even homework, the effort always produces desirable outcomes, but that doesn't make it any easier.

The biggest pitfall comes when we do miss a day or two of study time. Feelings of guilt, failure, or a desire to just quit can overpower us if we let it. However, what we must keep in mind is that guilt IS NOT of God. God may use conviction to draw you back into His will, but condemnation and guilt are never sent from the Father. Satan has effectively used these tools to derail Christians by the millions every year. I used to be a dedicated smoker (two packs a day), and when I was trying to quit I would frequently "fall off the wagon." Time and time again, the feelings of guilt and failure would make me throw in the towel and pick up the habit again. After spending some time hearing anointed teaching and preaching, I began to realize where this sense of condemnation was coming from, and it wasn't from God. Now I'm on to the enemy's tricks, and I refuse to let him steer my life anymore. Romans 8:1 reads: "*There is therefore now no condemnation to those who are in Christ Jesus, who do not walk according to the flesh, but according to the Spirit.*"

Prayer'th is'th just'th talk'th

"Our heavenly Father, we come before You today in supplication and with a contrite heart. We beseech You to meet us in our place of solitude and iniquity to impart Your unsearchable wisdom upon our very souls. The magnitude of Your blameless glory humbles us. Help us to overcome the original sin that plagues us, the sons of Adam, and lead us to our final abode in the bosom of Abraham through the magnanimous gift of Your grace. Help us to rest assured in the peace that passes all understanding and to stand elevated and erect under the pressure of our carnal flesh and the enemy of our soul. We live in eternal gratitude for the bountiful harvest that always remains for those who sup at Your table, and we ask for the authority to resist the fiery darts that seek to quench the rivers of living water that flow forth from Your elected. Amen."

Pretty huh? Eloquence and extensive use of vocabulary can definitely look nice and sound even better; but the real question is...where is your heart? I like to look at prayer the same way I look at a meal from a restaurant. The prayer that is given here has an awesome plate presentation, but what does the food taste like. I've been to several dining establishments that went out of their way to make the food appear to have been featured on the front cover of "Food Magazine," only to discover that the steak was rubbery and the vegetables were ice cold. On the other hand, an expertly made western omelet looks like a train wreck on the inside, but the different flavors combine to create a delicious delight.

God feeds on the prayer (communication) of His people; so what kind of taste are you going to leave in His mouth? Jesus illustrated this concept in the eighteenth chapter of Luke. He told a parable of a Pharisee and a tax collector both praying in the temple. A Pharisee was a teacher of the Old Testament Law. In Jesus' time, the Pharisees had become extremists, fundamentalists, and had elevated themselves above everyone else in their own eyes. A tax collector on the other hand, was considered the lowest stature of humanity that existed. Tax collectors were men that collected taxes from their fellow Jews for the Roman Empire, and made most of their living by collecting extra whenever they could. Jesus denounced the Pharisee's well-thought-out and eloquent (yet extremely conceited) prayer. However, He described the tax collectors prayer as an anguish-filled plea for mercy. Jesus declared in no uncertain terms which prayer was God-approved and which wasn't. Eloquence and vocabulary do not mean anything to God if our heart is not in our prayer.

Have you ever had a friend you genuinely cared about but would only hear from if they needed something? Every time this person's number would show up on the caller ID, you could rest assured that they needed money, someone to help them move, a ride somewhere, money…oh, did I already mention that? If you really care about this person you will still answer their calls, but isn't it frustrating to deal with someone like that? I wonder sometimes if God feels that way about some of His children. Even we regular church goers will neglect talking to our heavenly Father unless we are in dire straits. As soon as calamity befalls us, we are yelling "Oh God, help us in our time of need," but when life is running smoothly, we won't spend time communicating with the Master.

God loves us with an undying and perfect love, but He wants to be more than our *bail money*. Of course the choice is ours. We can call on God to constantly help us out of the hole that we've dug, or we can remain in steadfast communication and receive the guidance to walk away from the shovel before we begin digging. Two hour morning devotions are great, but a two minute check-in twenty times a day is even better. A constant line of communication is what He seeks and what our spirit needs. God doesn't want to be consulted on spiritual matters only. He wants to be involved in every aspect of our life, and believe me, if we give Him that type of involvement, He will guide our every step.

During His earthly ministry, Jesus actually gave his followers (and us) a model for effective prayer. In Mathew 6:9-13, Jesus says, "*In this manner, therefore, pray: Our Father in heaven, hallowed be Your name. Your kingdom come, Your will be done on earth as it is in heaven. Give us this day our daily bread. And forgive us our debts, as we forgive our debtors. And do not lead us into temptation, but deliver us from the evil one. For Yours is the kingdom and the power and the glory forever. Amen.*" Many churches and denominations take this command as a directive to recite this prayer verbatim, and I don't believe that there is anything wrong with this; but I look at this prayer as an example of the priorities when communicating with God. Let's dissect this prayer and see what God's only Son thinks is most important when talking with the Master.

"Our Father in heaven, hallowed be Your name." The first section of this model instructs us to recognize that God is our Father and to worship Him. The word worship means to bow down before someone as an act of submission or reverence. Authentic worship is pleasing to God, but don't take my word for it. In John 4:23, Jesus declares, *"But the hour is coming, and now is, when the true worshipers will worship the Father in spirit and truth, for the Father is seeking such to worship Him."* True worship maintains the focus of Who God is, and what God has done. Genuine worship for Him Who sits on the throne of heaven will become evident in our attitudes, actions, and especially our prayers when we truly realize that on our own, we are capable of nothing. For many people, the idea of worship brings to mind simply singing and praising God, but as Christians our life should be a picture of Godly worship. We give this worship in many different ways including vocal praise and thanksgiving, returning our tithe to God, giving of our substance (money, material possessions, etc.) to people or ministries, and working (serving) in our local house of worship. Giving honor and reverence to Him in every way and on a daily basis is what He deserves and what we were put on earth to accomplish.

"Your kingdom come, Your will be done on earth as it is in heaven." In this passage we are compelled to pray for God to increase His kingdom on

earth and to express our desire that His will be accomplished down here as mightily as it is in the heavenly kingdom. We need to recognize that in praying for His will to be done on earth like it is in heaven, we are acknowledging that God's will is often ignored on earth. While He is sovereign (having supreme authority and power), He gave us free will. He wanted us to choose to live for Him, not be robots that have no choice. And in case you haven't noticed, we can make some pretty bone-headed decisions sometimes. This really isn't any different from Bible times. In Acts 7:51, the author (historically thought to be Luke, the physician and companion of Paul) said, "*You stiff-necked and uncircumcised in heart and ears! You always resist the Holy Spirit; as your fathers did, so do you.*" All too often we give no place to God's will and seek our own interests. However, in our prayer life we should always beseech the Master to help us line up our desires with His will.

"*Give us this day our daily bread.*" Jesus declares that it is good and proper to request and believe for our daily needs to be met. He is our provider and sustainer, and we must always rely on him for our provision. God is our heavenly Father, and no father wants to see his children lacking. He wants us to ask Him for our every need. James 4:2 says, "*You lust and do not have. You murder and covet and cannot obtain. You fight and war. Yet you do not have because you do not ask.*" However, believing for what you have asked is just as important as the request itself. In his gospel account, Mark quotes Jesus in the eleventh chapter and the twenty fourth verse saying, "*Therefore I say to you, whatever things you ask when you pray, believe that you receive them, and you will have them.*"

"*And forgive us our debts as we forgive our debtors.*" In this passage, Jesus stresses the importance of living in repentance and forgiveness. In our prayers, we need to always ask God for forgiveness for sins. Being a Christian does not make you immune to the yielding to temptation. We are called to try to live a perfect life knowing that we cannot accomplish the duty. However, God is quick to forgive a repentant heart. The key to true repentance is to make a change in the way we live. One of the keys to receiving God's forgiveness is to be quick to forgive others as well. In Mark 11:25, Jesus declares, "*And whenever you stand praying, if you have anything against anyone, forgive him, that your Father in heaven may also forgive you your trespasses.*"

"*And do not lead us into temptation, but deliver us from the evil one.*" While researching this phrase, I went through a bit of a struggle. I know that God's word never contradicts itself, but this is what it seems to do in this passage. James 1:13 very clearly states "*Let no one say when he is tempted, 'I am tempted by God,' for God cannot be tempted by evil, nor does He Himself tempt anyone."* This caused me to dig a little deeper into what was being conveyed in this section of the prayer. What I found was encouraging and insightful. While God does not, in fact, ever tempt us, He will allow us to go through temptation to strengthen our faith. He even led His only Son Jesus into the wilderness to be tempted by the enemy. After all, there would never be any victory if there were never any trials. However, Jesus is telling us to pray that God will help us to never enter *into* any temptations. In other words, we are told to ask and believe God to help us withstand and not yield to temptations, but to stand firm and deny the enemy any place in our lives. In I Corinthians 10:13, Paul writes, *"No temptation has overtaken you except such as is common to man; but God is faithful, who will not allow you to be tempted beyond what you are able, but with the temptation will also make the way of escape, that you may be able to bear it."*

"For Yours is the kingdom and the power and the glory forever. Amen." Once again, Jesus stresses the importance of recognizing who God is and giving Him all of the glory He is due. To worship God is what we were made to do, so let us constantly remember to start and end in an attitude of humble worship. Our prayers need to always reflect our recognition that God is worthy of all honor and reverence. In fact, in the book of Luke, some of the

religious leaders of Jesus' time were irritated at His followers expressing their adoration and worship in loud voices. These Pharisees asked Jesus to tell his disciples to pipe down. In Luke 19:40 it proclaims, *"But He answered and said to them, 'I tell you that if these should keep silent, the stones would immediately cry out.'"* God will get His worship one way or the other; but as His followers, we should always desire to be the ones to give Him the praise of which He is worthy.

Prayer, just like studying the word of God, requires discipline at times. We live in a fast paced and sometimes stressful world that seems to require us to rush from one thing to the next. However, if we take a bit of time and examine our busy lives, we will discover that we always seem to "make time" for the things that are the most important to us. There is absolutely nothing more important than communication with our Master, and our prayer time needs to be treated as priority number one. There is no job, family member, promotion, hobby, or pastime that can come before our relationship with God. He requires being first in all areas of our lives; and c'mon, I think we owe it to Him.

Habits become passions

Have you ever heard of the concept of "runner's high"? That term has been around for decades, but until I started writing this book, I had never been interested enough to look into it. Runner's high is a release of endorphins in the athlete's body that allows athletes to go far beyond their normal physical limit. In fact, the athlete experiencing this release of endorphins often feels no pain or fatigue at all. Considering the fact that I am somewhat of a large mammal, I find the whole idea of runner's high rather dubious and even a bit creepy (I had to look up the word "run" just to refresh myself on *its* meaning). I have been assured by reliable sources however, that it does exist. I have heard bodybuilders and weight room junkies talk about similar experiences while lifting weights or working out. However, the universal truth behind these phenomena is that they don't exist in the beginning. In fact, there were an extensive number of regurgitation and charley-horse stories that earmarked the first few weeks or even months of these athletes' training.

What I'm trying to say is that establishing habits is difficult in the beginning. Part of the reason for this is the difficulty in replacing old habits. Starting to walk thirty minutes on a treadmill during your lunch break is hard enough, but you're also using this new healthy habit to replace the "Gorge and Go" Chinese buffet that is your normal lunch location for the last two years. This makes the process doubly difficult. Normally, your heart, your mind, and your body are constantly at odds about everything. But in this one area they are in complete harmony: routine is good. Routine decreases stress, it creates an easily attainable agenda, and it gives your life a stability that is hard to find. Unfortunately, altering your routine increases stress, adds unknown variables to life, and creates a sense of unpredictability. Replacing old habits with new ones is not as easy as it sounds, but it is necessary for creating a new and spiritually healthy routine.

In my own personal life, I struggled with finding time to spend with God and with His word. General consensus with the experts is that early morning was the best time period for serious "God time." I found this time slot extremely difficult to put into practice. I worked second shift and didn't normally get off work until 1:00 am. When I tried to read the Bible and pray in the morning, I generally found myself dozing off or mentally wandering around. This did precious little for me and probably less for God. I then tried for mid-day. I was much more alert and focused, but I found myself worrying about everything that I needed to get done before work. I eventually settled on a late night prayer and study time. After work I am always alert, the house is quiet, and I have the needed peace to read and to pray. To be honest, most of this book was written in the wee hours of the morning. It's when I'm at my sharpest and most focused. What I'm saying is this, choosing the best time for *you* can go a long way toward establishing a successful routine. A successful routine will blossom into an ingrained habit, and an ingrained habit can become a burning passion when your desire for spiritual growth is constant. The Old Testament prophet Daniel, even when faced with dire consequences, prayed to God three times a day "*as was his custom since early days*" (Daniel 6:10). He did this knowing full well that it was against the law at the time and that the punishment for this crime was death. Do you think his habit had become passion?

Chapter 3

<u>Joy Walks On Busy Feet</u>

Walk is an action verb...So Act!!

Numerous times thus far you have heard me mention the phrase
"our walk with God." There are hundreds of ways that I could have phrased
this expression for relationship with the Father, but I chose walk because it is
the most appropriate. Of the very small handful of things that I retained from
my high school physics class, one concept that has stuck with me is that of
inertia. A body at rest tends to stay at rest, and a body in motion tends to stay
in motion. A perfect example of this concept is an automobile stuck in the
snow or mud. You can get five large guys pushing it from a dead stop and it
will hardly move. However, if you can start rocking the car in its tracks and
add that forward momentum to the push, you'll usually free it. This is not
only true of inanimate objects but people as well. In fact, humans are
progressively harder to get moving the longer they are at rest. No matter how
stale and stagnant things in our life become, there is still a comfort in sticking

to a routine. No one is crazy about change. The old phrase "stuck in their old ways" is more revealing than you might think. Stuck is a fairly apt word for people who never change, adapt, or grow.

Accepting Jesus into your life as Lord and Master is a pretty big change, but far too many people halt their progress right there. I'm no Bible scholar or seminary-schooled theologian, but I can tell you one thing: this idea of "get saved then sit around and wait for God's return" does not please the Father. The author of the book of Hebrews scolds this group of early Christians to which he is writing about this very thing. Chapter 5:12-14 reads, "*For though by this time you ought to be teachers, you need someone to teach you again the first principles of the oracles of God; and you have come to need milk and not solid food.*"This is a pretty harsh rebuke when you think about it. The author is calling these believers spiritual babies even though they have been in church long enough to be pastors and teachers by now. This really gives us a good glimpse of the heart of the Father. God expects us to grow and mature in Him continually. In Colossians 1:10, the apostle Paul writes, "*that you may walk worthy of the Lord, fully pleasing Him, being fruitful in every good work and increasing in the knowledge of God.*" We are specifically instructed by God's Word to be constantly maturing and growing in the wisdom and knowledge of God. The Master is never satisfied with stagnation, and we shouldn't be either.

Have you ever been in a place of darkness, so total, that you couldn't see your hand in front of your face? When you finally encounter a light, it is so bright that it nearly blinds you. That light is all you can see. It may even cause pain until your senses can learn to cope with it. Receiving salvation is much like this. When we were still unsaved, we were wandering in complete darkness. The light of Jesus consumes us after we receive Him. For a while, it is all we can see and all that matters. However, as time passes we become accustomed to the light. If we stay in that same pool of light long enough, we start to take that light for granted. We are no longer as thankful for it. This may sound like a degenerate state of mind, but it really isn't.

According to Genesis 1:26, we have been created in God's likeness and image, and God is never satisfied with the status quo. This is not to downplay salvation of course. Our salvation is a free gift that is the absolute picture of God's grace and mercy. However, we must seek out God's will for our lives and must act on His wishes. No amount of sitting in church can be a substitute for living out the Master's instructions. We can hear anointed sermons, take pages of notes, and have whole media libraries full of CDs and

DVDs, but if we never put into practice what we are learning, it does us no good.

This is a major problem with millions of Christians today. We tend to think if we go to church and hear good teaching on biblical principles we are doing our job. This is a major fallacy that is pointed out in the New Testament. James 1:22-25 reads, "*But be doers of the word, and not hearers only, deceiving yourselves. For if anyone is a hearer of the word and not a doer, he is like a man observing his natural face in a mirror; for he observes himself, goes away, and immediately forgets what kind of man he was. But he who looks into the perfect law of liberty and continues in it, and is not a forgetful hearer, but a doer of the work, this one will be blessed in what he does.*" How do we put what we learn into practice? The key is to walk in all of the light we have. In other words, what we know and understand, we must practice and do. As long as you are firmly rooted in the pool of light that you are in, you will never be given new light.

The best analogy of which I can think is a motion sensor light. If you stand still, then only the light for that particular area will be illuminated. However, when we exhaust all of the light around us and step out toward the waiting darkness, the next set of lights comes on. Our relationship with Jesus is much like this scenario. If we stay truly hungry to know Him, then we will be doers of what we know (no matter how little that is). If we are faithful to do everything we know, then God leads us on to new revelation and more light. The more we mature and grow to know Him, the more light He will give to us. The intimidating part is reaching the end of the light and taking that first step into seeming darkness. That is the definition of faith: stepping into the unknown but believing God will work things out. We have to take that first step if we want to please Him. Hebrews 11:6 says, "*But without faith it is impossible to please Him, for he who comes to God must believe that He is, and that He is a rewarder of those who diligently seek Him.*" You see? When you become a child of God, you are required to live by faith, and it will take faith to leave your comfort zone. Nothing pleases the Father more than watching His people step out into the darkness guided only by His leading, and their absolute trust in His faithfulness.

Work: the four letter word

So now we are saved, sanctified, washed in the blood and live in full confidence that construction on our heavenly mansion has begun in earnest. It is time to put it on cruise control and wait on God to collect us whenever He's ready, right? Well, let's put it this way: If you finally got the job of your dreams, you wouldn't show up to punch the clock and then sit around waiting for quitting time would you? Wait, don't answer that. Let me re-phrase. Your boss doesn't expect you to punch the clock and then sit around waiting for quitting time, does he/she? I'm afraid that too many people's dream job would involve doing just that, but we are obviously expected to do the job we were hired to do. If allowed to go on a tangent about Christians showing character and integrity in his or her workplace, I would have to add a few extra chapters in this book. To keep it short and sweet: your employer hired you to give them eight hours of honest work a day, so that's what you better be giving them. Anything less would be a poor representation of Christ and the way He has called His people to live with integrity. We are to do everything we set out to do like we were doing it for God Himself. Paul writes, "*And whatever you do, do it heartily, as to the Lord and not as to men,*" Colossians 3:23.

Maturing in God will also involve the "w" word; Work. Your relationship with Him will require diligence, hard work, routinely denying your natural desires, and a constant flow of changed plans. Don't give up on this chapter just yet. I know that it doesn't sound like rainbows and unicorns so far, but I will tell you this: the rewards for this kind of relationship with

God are mind blowing. And they are not solely eternal rewards for your soul, but tangible hands-on rewards right here on earth.

In the book of Hebrews, chapter 6 and verses 10-12, the author writes, "*For God is not unjust to forget your work and labor of love which you have shown toward His name, in that you have ministered to the saints, and do minister. And we desire that each one of you show the same diligence to the full assurance of hope until the end, that you do not become sluggish, but imitate those who through faith and patience inherit the promises.*" The question that we need to ask ourselves is this: Does God expect something from us after we're saved? According to these verses, we would have to answer that question with a big fat "you betcha." Salvation is a free gift from the Father, and far be it from me to ever downplay the richest of God's gifts, but this isn't the end of our story. We're not called to be a church seat warmer, but to be a worker for His kingdom. I'd like to spend some time breaking down these scriptures and deciphering God's will for every one of us in this area.

"*For God is not unjust to forget your work and labor of love which you have shown toward His name, in that you have ministered to the saints, and do minister.*" The Master expects us to work. We who are living in today's society, especially in the United States, tend to look at the word "work" as a vile and nasty four letter word. To many of us, work is another way of saying "getting underpaid for hard labor done for someone else's benefit." Even many Christians equate work with sweat, misery and dread. I believe we need some real mind renewing on the concept of work. This next statement may turn your world upside down, but it is biblical and I will prove it to you. God invented work. There it is, in all of its unabashed glory. In Genesis 2:2, the Bible reads, "*And on the seventh day God ended His **work** which He had done, and He rested on the seventh day from all His **work** which He had done*" (emphasis mine). He labored for His creations and put work into making the heavens and the earth. Not only this, but God charged the first man (Adam) to do work, even before Adam's fall into sin. Genesis 2:15 states, "*Then the Lord God took the man and put him in the Garden of Eden to tend and keep it.*" And I can say with all certainty that He has not changed His mind on this subject. He expects us to work, not only in our natural life but in our spiritual life as well.

Now there is a pretty good reason that so many people detest the idea of work. It is because the majority of us are not doing the work that God is calling us to do. I'm not singling out the non-believers here, but I am talking about Christians as well. Don't believe for one second that unbelievers have cornered the market on dead-end jobs, broken dreams and settling for second, third, or fourth best. Look around and you will see many dedicated Christian people who are dragging themselves through life with jobs they hate, ministries that remain unfulfilled, and life goals that seem unattainable.

Let's imagine for a few minutes that you are a wonderfully gifted pianist. The notes, the keys, the progressions, they all come easily to you. However, you have no idea about this talent of yours. You only know that you desire to be involved in the musical arts. You get hired as part of an orchestra, and you have to play the tuba. You show up for work every day, but you loathe the tuba. You have to put in far more hours of practice than you think is reasonable, your cheeks hurt every day from blowing, and you despise the sound that the tuba makes. You are miserable at work. Every day you come home and complain about your job to anyone who will listen. You pray every night that God will help you feel better about your job and allow you to enjoy it more. All the while, God is doing everything, short of sending you an email, to let you know that you have been graced as a pianist, not a tuba player. But of course, you *know* that God is very interested in your spiritual life, but He doesn't meddle in your personal affairs, so you don't take the time to listen.

This sounds overly melodramatic and tragic, but far too many of us are living exactly this way. This is why so many of us develop hives at the sound of the word *work*. However, it doesn't have to be this way. Our scripture from Hebrews tells us that God doesn't forget our work or labor. Proverbs 3:6 declares, "*In all your ways acknowledge Him, and He shall direct your paths*." God is just as interested in what we are doing for a living as He is in what we do in church or in our ministry. If we seek Him about everything that goes on in our life, He is faithful to help us and keep us on the path of His will. This includes putting us into the line of work that will best accomplish His purpose for us. This is not to say that we will be wildly excited to get to our job every day or we will be so thoroughly elated with our profession that we would do it for free. But there is a definite sense of fulfillment when doing work that we know we are called to do. Even a seemingly mundane or tedious job can be immeasurable satisfying if it is, indeed, where God called you to be.

Natural work aside, we also need to be working in the kingdom of God. When completing work for God and for His children, we need to be even more diligent. Nothing but our "A Game" will suffice for kingdom work. Have you ever heard someone say "I don't care what you do to me, but don't EVER mess with my kids"? If you're a parent, then you can certainly relate to this sentiment. Well, God takes the exact same view when looking at His children. He takes it personal when you mess with His saints. And on the flip side, anything done for His kids will be long remembered and amply rewarded. God is a spirit. He doesn't need help with His mortgage or to have His car paid off. With the exception of praise and worship, there isn't too much we can do to honor Him personally, but we can honor His children. Work done for the body of the church (the believers) will always hold a special place in the Master's heart.

"And we desire that each one of you show the same diligence to the full assurance of hope until the end." We keep seeing this word "diligent" pop up in our conversation and in scripture. What does this word mean in the context of our passage? Contrary to what many people think, the Bible was not written in the English language. It was translated from Hebrew (most of the Old Testament) and Greek (most of the New Testament). Many times in the Hebrew or Greek language, a word will have many different meanings or can be translated into several words that we might use. The scribes or monks, who translated the word of God into English, used the context of the passage to determine which meaning to use for a particular word. Diligence is a word that has many meanings; but when viewing all of them you will get a more complete picture of what was being conveyed by the apostle Paul. In Strong's

Talking Greek and Hebrew dictionary, it explains that the word diligence comes from the Greek word *spoudē*. This word can be translated to include all of the following: with passion, earnestness, carefulness, with haste, and early. So we not only need to be obedient and hardworking, but we need to be prompt and on-time.

Procrastination is one of the most effective tools of the enemy to hinder God's work. This attitude of "well, I'll get around to it" or "I might have time tomorrow" is something that we need to eliminate in order to fully live in God's plan for our life and His church. Satan often can't get you to give up on your aspirations and plans for God, so he does the next best thing: he encourages you to put it off. Our busy lives can be a seemingly legitimate reason for putting things off; but sometimes we need to step back and analyze what we're so busy with, and determine if it is really worth putting God's things on hold.

Once you begin to exhibit diligence in His work, you need to keep it up until the end. Far too many of us get started on things but we fade out before it's done. Paul encourages the saints in Romans chapter 8 and verse 11, "*but now you also must complete the doing of it; that as there was a readiness to desire it, so there also may be a completion out of what you have.*" Jesus likewise warned the crowds following Him of the same issue. In the gospel account of Luke, the twenty eighth through the thirtieth verses of chapter 14 reads, "*For which of you, intending to build a tower, does not sit down first and count the cost, whether he has enough to finish it? Lest, after he has laid the foundation, and is not able to finish, all who see it begin to mock him, saying 'This man began to build and was not able to finish.'*" Here, Jesus is stressing not only the importance of finishing a task, but also stresses not projecting a foolish image in front of others. He wants us not only to be finishers of what we start, but He wants us to present a picture of wisdom to those who are watching. And believe me; people are always watching anyone who professes Christ as their Savior.

"… *that you do not become sluggish, but imitate those who through faith and patience inherit the promises.* "The last part of this scripture holds an important key for staying strong, staying on course, and staying accountable. He says "*imitate those who through faith and patience inherit the promises.*" I cannot stress enough the paramountcy of having Godly mentors in your life. We all serve the one true Shepherd (Jesus). And if we are obeying the Word of God's command and attending church, then we all should have an under-shepherd (pastor). But it is vitally important to have additional mentors and Godly relationships in our life as well.

I have witnessed many Christians with the "me and God, and that's all I need" mentality. Most of these people don't even attend a house of worship, or if they do, they don't serve in any capacity in the church. I'm not saying these people don't have relationships with God. They may be saved, sanctified and heading to the pearly gates, but they are not experiencing everything God has for them. The Bible makes it clear in numerous passages that God created us to be in relationship with people. I don't necessarily mean romantic relationships or marriage, but those are certainly part of the picture for most people. Relationships with family, members of your church family, neighbors, co-workers; all of these relationships are important to God and should be important to you as well. However, right now I want to focus on Godly mentors and what I will be calling from here on out, *faith friends.*

Ear ticklers need not apply

There are a lot of people out there who are more than happy to fill your head with pleasant ideas, fawn over your accomplishments, and offer many hollow words of praise. This type of person can make you feel good sometimes, but they are not what you really need. You need a mentor. Mentor is a word from the Greek word, also Mentor, meaning *wise advisor.* In this context, that definition is fitting along with Merriam-Webster's definition: a trusted counselor or guide. Many people say they want a mentor, but they really want a buddy. They want someone they can impress with their spiritual progress and growth. However, a true mentor will not be impressed by you. They will often speak things to you that you will not want to hear. They will not be hateful or rude, but they will call you on your faults and push you to rise above your nature. A mentor will commonly butt heads with you.

King Solomon wrote about spiritual mentors in Proverbs 27:17. It reads, "*As iron sharpens iron, so a man sharpens the countenance of his friend.*" When using iron to sharpen iron, there is friction involved...friction so intense there may be sparks. However, both swords involved become sharper and **more useful** in the process. This is because both elements are being used in the correct way. The mentor is using the God-given ability and calling to tutor the student, and the student is being obedient and learning what God desires them to know through the wisdom and anointing of the mentor. In Romans 15:14, Paul writes to the saints in Rome, "*Now I myself am confident concerning you, my brethren, that you are also full of goodness, filled with all knowledge, able also to admonish one another.*"So as we grow and mature under the tutelage of a mentor, we are being sculpted by God into mentors ourselves. And that should always be the goal: to become a mentor to others.

What does a Godly mentor look like?

How do I find one?

A mentor won't look any different than anyone else in physical appearance, but what's on the outside matters little. Their lifestyle and conduct will stand out as the identifying markers. They will be people who respect the things of God, respect the men and women that God placed in a position of authority in the church, and will show genuine interest in people. They won't be haphazard about church attendance and they won't be seat warmers who don't serve in the church. In other words, they will be spiritually mature. When seeking a mentor, you must be diligent in prayer. If you ask God in prayer and are earnest and authentic in your request, God will bring someone into your path. However, your first test will be recognizing that person, and cultivating that relationship. A good prospective mentor will not, right away, eagerly agree to step into that role. They will question you about your motives, your commitment, and your honesty. Only when satisfied, that you are serious about growth and maturity, will that person commit to you.

I would like to add a word here about accountability. A person cannot be a good mentor if you cannot be honest with them and let them hold you accountable. Their ability to be an accountability partner hinges on whether you will have the integrity to admit your mistakes. In the sixth chapter of Galatians, verses one and two, Paul writes, "*Brethren, if a man is overtaken in any trespass, you who are spiritual restore such a one in a spirit of gentleness, considering yourself lest you also be tempted. Bear one another's burdens, and so fulfill the law of Christ.*" Your mentor cannot restore you and help you if you won't be completely open with them. Transparency is vital in an accountability relationship.

At the time of this writing, my wife and I are seeking this very thing in our local church. I have been at this church for almost five years and it is where I met my beautiful wife. We are involved in many different aspects of service there. She leads praise and worship for the elementary grades in Sunday school classes as well as being heavily involved in the Visual Arts team. I sing on the Worship Arts Team and I am frequently a part of the holiday stage productions and special services too. We lead a small group book study on Sunday nights and have been the host home for many youth functions. Yes, we are busy, but we need guidance and spiritual direction as much or more than anyone. As single people in the past, we both had mentors, and we maintain those connections. But we both feel like we need to find a couple that can act as our mentors for this stage of our life and growth. We are seeking God and praying that He will send a mature married couple into our path that will help to hold us accountable. Neither of us is perfect and we both have areas in which we struggle. We both feel we need accountability. Everyone reading this right now can probably think of two or three prominent religious figures who have been involved in scandals. Sexual promiscuity, fund embezzlement, child abuse - the list goes on. In almost all of these cases, had these public figures valued and sought after accountability in their life, there would be no scandal to talk about. God brings people into our lives to encourage, help, admonish, and discipline us. Use them!!!

Now a faith friend is a bit different than a mentor. Fellowship (that's a Christian buzzword for stuffing your face and enjoying the company of others) plays a much bigger role in this type of relationship. My wife Brandi and I, have several couples and single friends who we consider our faith friends. We get together, always over a ridiculously fattening meal, and just have fun. I hear some of the religious people harrumphing, but it IS possible (and preferable) to have fun being a Christian. That doesn't mean you don't ever get counsel, cry on a shoulder, or talk about the word of God. In fact, your faith friends need to be people of like mind and like faith. I know that our friends who hold this role are people of faith that we respect. However, there is a lot more give and take with these relationships. We encourage them at times and other times we need to be built up ourselves. We pour into them, they pour into us. And we have a lot of laughs along the way. There are times when I have had a rough day and I feel like the enemy has just stomped me into a mud hole. I'll call one of my faith friends just to hear him tell me that I am an overcomer...that God always causes me to triumph...that He who has begun a good work in me will complete it.

It has been my experience that finding good faith friends can be just as challenging as finding a good mentor. Being an introvert, I tend to have more difficulty finding friends period. However, the older I've become, the more I've come to recognize the foundational principles of God's word working in everyday life. One of the foundational building blocks of the Bible is the concept of sowing and reaping. Genesis 8:22 reads, "*While the earth remains, seedtime and harvest, cold and heat, winter and summer, and day and night shall not cease.*" God is telling us that along with the turning of the seasons, the inevitability of day turning to night and then back again, and the temperature rising and falling, seed time and harvest (sowing and reaping) will always occur. And of course seed always produces after its own kind. You will never plant tomato seeds and grow turnips from it. Keeping this basic principle in mind, we are to sow in the area in which we are hoping to reap. Once I latched on to this idea, things got easier for me. If you need a friend, be friendly. Once I stopped being the recluse and involved myself in small groups and service teams at the church, I started making friends.

In fact, attending a marriage class was how I met my bride. While this is not a marriage book, I will give all of you who are married a little advice. Find a biblical based marriage class and attend it. It doesn't even have to be *your* church sponsoring it. The marriage class at our church welcomed people from all houses of worship and denominations to attend. Don't wait until you have problems in your marriage to invest in your marriage. This goes for singles as well. I was single when I started attending these marriage meetings because I wanted to prepare and to make myself the best potential husband possible. Brandi was there doing the same thing. Marriage is the first human relationship that God established on this earth, so you need to take it as seriously as He does.

Of course, there are many other types of relationships that need to be built up and nurtured. God sent His Son to die for mankind. To the heavenly Father, there is nothing that exists more important than people. We need to cultivate the same attitude. You're not always going to get along with everyone and that's okay. Some people just rub you the wrong way. You will always have to deal with difficult people; and God's word does not say that you have to trust them, be buddies with them, or put your heart in their hands. However, you do have to love them. God does. When we can come to the realization that God created people in His image, it is much easier to love people despite their faults. Those faults and weaknesses were not planted there by God. The enemy holds sway with a large percentage of the people on this planet, but that is where the blame needs to rest; at the feet of the enemy. God's creation (man) is perfect. Satan and sin have corrupted us, so don't be too quick to let your negative feelings influence how you treat someone. You don't have to become best friends with someone to love and respect them as one of God's creations. God doesn't make mistakes! In Jeremiah 1:5, the prophet writes, *"Before I formed you in the womb I knew you…"* While God is talking to Jeremiah here, this stands true for all of us. God has a great future planned for each of us as long as we will submit to His will. People are the greatest investments we can make in this life, and we need to get behind God's vision which He spells out in 2 Peter 3:9. Peter writes, *"The Lord is not slack concerning His promise, as some count slackness, but is longsuffering toward us, not willing that any should perish but that all should come to repentance."* He has patience with us, so we need to be patient with others.

Faith: the decoder ring for God's will

Okay, I'm about to do a grave disservice to one of the most immense and important concepts in the whole Bible by only dedicating one part of one chapter to it. Many have written books twice the size of this publication on the subject matter of faith, and they still haven't scratched the surface of everything there is to know about it. The only justification I have is that faith is necessary **to** and interwoven **in** every subject I've discussed thus far and will be an integral part of everything to come.

While this section may be short, having and using faith is the heartbeat of everything I've written. The author of Hebrews explains it better than I can. A few pages back I used this scripture but it bears repeating, *"But without faith it is impossible to please Him, for he who comes to God must believe that He is, and that He is a rewarder of those who diligently seek Him."* So you see, God cannot be pleased unless you are using faith to do whatever He asks you to do. When you asked God to come into your heart you were doing it by faith. You had to believe with no visible evidence that Jesus was entering your heart and that you were forgiven. Jesus wasn't standing in front of you physically. You didn't pour Him some coffee and sit down in your breakfast nook to talk. You didn't even get a text from the

Father reading, "Oh My Me, traffic is crazy. B there in 10." You had to believe that what you read or heard about God and salvation was true and have faith that He was in heaven listening to you. By faith you let Him in and gave Him control of your life. This first experience of faith won't be your last if you continue to live for God. As you could tell from that scripture, God expects us to utilize our faith every day and grow in it continually.

Dictionary.com defines faith as "strong or unshakeable belief in something, especially without proof or evidence." Merriam-Webster defines faith as "strong belief or trust in someone or something." However, the Bible defines faith in Hebrews 11:1 reading, *"Now faith is the substance of things hoped for, the evidence of things not seen."* As always, the word of God breaks things down to give us just what we need in order to understand. Faith is evident in our lives from the moment we begin comprehension as an infant. As babies, we cried for food and mom hurried to feed us. After seeing that a few times, we had faith that even if mom wasn't in the same room and we could not see her, if we cried, she would appear and give us food. As we grew, we continued to put our faith in certain people, things, or events. If you stay up until 4:30 am and all around you is pitch black, you still have faith that in an hour or so, the sun will rise. Experience has taught you that event is faithful. It doesn't fail. Some people are the same way. If they tell you they will be somewhere at a certain time, they will be there. They don't have to show up before you believe. You have learned their character, and their character makes them worthy of trust.

Once you have made a decision to live your life for Christ, there is a time period of getting to know God's character. The best way to learn is to read the Bible and learn about Him by reading about Him. (If you don't believe that the Bible is one-hundred percent true and is the inspired word of God Himself, then you are fooling yourself about your own Christian conversion. As a true Christian, we don't get to pick and choose what parts of the Bible we believe and what we don't. It's either all true, or none of it.)

As you learn about God's love for His people and His faithfulness, you begin to trust in Him more and more. Romans 12:3 says, "*For I say, through the grace given to me, to everyone who is among you, not to think of himself more highly than he ought to think, but to think soberly, as God has dealt to each one a measure of faith*" So each of us has a measure of faith, but that faith needs to be nurtured and made to grow and mature. No one starts off their Christian life as a giant in faith. We all start off as babies learning the ropes of this new life. A brand new Christian knows only the fundamentals. God wants a relationship with me, He has forgiven my sins, and He has saved me from being eternally separated from Him. However, as we study His word and listen to good Christian teaching, we discover that God has a calling or a purpose for our lives and we need to grow in faith to accomplish this purpose.

How does faith grow? Well, that's the million dollar question that needs answered. Well, how does faith *in a person* grow? As we learn their honesty and integrity, we begin to trust that what they say, they will do. Some aspects of our faith in God grow much the same way; however, after some maturity on our part, we are expected to reverse the process. That may have sounded a bit confusing, but I will explain.

When dealing with people, we learn that they can be trusted therefore we place our faith in them. God also wants us to discover His faithfulness. However, His goal is for us to have this genuine trust in His character and integrity *before* we ever have any proof. This sounds pretty unreasonable for someone just getting to know Him. Fortunately, He won't put the cart in front of the horse. God is very merciful with spiritual babies. He understands the lack of knowledge that we start off with and will often show us His goodness and graciousness without much interaction from us. The same way that a mother would not place a ten-ounce ribeye in front of an infant, God won't expect us to digest the deeper aspects of His word before we learn to drink milk. A baby needs to learn to take nourishment from his bottle before he learns to eat solid food. In the beginning, we won't be held accountable for much more than being fed. As we learn scripture and mature out of spiritual infancy, we will start to be able to chew and digest more solid spiritual food.

Learning to exercise our faith is one of these meals. God will start requiring more out of our faith than just sitting back with an open mouth. Eventually, the "seeing is believing" will have to be replaced with genuine faith. With God, we need to put the believing in front of the seeing. Just like definition of the word as revealed in the book of Hebrews, real faith is belief and trust when we see no evidence of occurrence. The old adage of "I'll believe it when I see it" doesn't require faith at all. Every non-believer lives by this rule because there is no risk. Believers are called to something different. Like the example from earlier in this chapter, true faith will take a step into the darkness believing the next light will illuminate. This is the kind of trust that pleases God immensely. The more often we are able to put this into practice, the easier it will become to trust in God in even more situations.

I'm sure there are many people reading this wondering if it's even worth it to mature in our faith. It sure sounds easier to sit back and let our teachers, preachers, and mentors spoon feed us. We're still saved right? Why go through the maturation process at all? The short answer is simple; God desires us to grow. I mean, that is the main point of living for God anyway, right? We want to please Him, right? Jesus is pretty clear on that in John 14:15 which reads, "*If you love Me, keep My commandments.*" And in Hebrews 5 verses 12-14, the author writes, "*For though by this time you ought to be teachers, you need someone to teach you again the first principles of the oracles of God; and you have come to need milk and not solid food. For everyone who partakes only of milk is unskilled in the word of righteousness, for he is a babe. But solid food belongs to those who are of full age, that is, those who by reason of use have their senses exercised to discern both good and evil.*"God was not happy that His church was full of people that should be teaching others, but instead still needed to be taught the fundamentals because they weren't maturing. His desire was and is quite clear. He wants a church that is mature and ready to put their faith in Him.

If that reason isn't enough, although it should be, there are other reasons to develop in faith. Let's not forget the second part of the verse from Hebrews 11, "*... and that He is a rewarder of those who diligently seek Him.*" God wants to reward His children the same as any father does, and His blessings are on a monumental scale! Because He is a God who is concerned with every detail of our lives, even those that are seemingly mundane, we are expected to use our faith in every arena of life.

Speaking personally, I release my faith on things that unbelievers would probably consider petty or trivial. I not only stand on God's word and His promises for things like healing, provision, and furthering God's kingdom; but I believe Him for things like decent sleep, good parking spaces, decent weather for outdoor plans, and peace with quarrelsome family members. This may sound ridiculous to some, but I believe that my good Father in heaven wants me to experience favor in this life and I have scripture to back it up! In Psalms 84:11, the Psalmist writes, *"For the Lord God is a sun and shield; The Lord will give grace and glory; No good thing will He withhold from those who walk uprightly."* The apostle Paul writes in 2 Corinthians 9:8, *"And God is able to make all grace abound toward you, that you, always having all sufficiency in all things, may have an abundance for every good work."* That is one of the huge rewards of living a life of faith; God wants to see me prosper even more than I do!

Other than pleasing God and reaping the rewards, there is one other important reason to develop in faith: impacting others. In Acts 13:47, Luke writes, *"For so the Lord has commanded us: 'I have set you as a light to the*

Gentiles, That you should be for salvation to the ends of the earth'."

Unbelievers should be able to look at us and think, "Wow, I want what they have." Growing in faith and maturing in God will produce results that are hard to deny. Living by faith won't produce perfection or a life free of troubles, but it will create a man or woman who knows how to come out of their troubles victoriously. The problems and cares of this life can't keep an individual of faith down. God never promised us utopia down here on earth, but He did promise us we would triumph over any trial or test that life could throw at us. Paul writes in I Corinthians 15:57, "*But thanks be to God, who gives us the victory through our Lord Jesus Christ.*" This is the kind of person that unbelievers need to see! There is no better representation of a Christian than someone who is healed, has their needs met, and has joy!

   Faith not only needs to grow, but it needs to be used properly. Naturally as faith grows and matures, we will learn how to use or apply it. Of course this knowledge doesn't just appear overnight. We must discover it through prayer and study. Paul writes to Timothy in his second letter to the young pastor in chapter 2 verse 15 saying, *"Be diligent to present yourself approved to God, a worker who does not need to be ashamed, rightly dividing the word of truth."* We must study God's word and in doing so, we will learn how to properly use our faith. Over and over again, I hear stories of people becoming bitter, becoming discouraged, or simply walking away from God because of misplaced, impatient, or dyslexic faith. Each of these misuses of faith can be avoided if we adhere to what I call the three fundamentals of faith.

Hear from God

The first rule is the one that is most commonly broken; hear from God. It is so simple yet so often skipped. We cannot have faith and believe for something that isn't God's will. (Well, I guess we can, but it's not going to turn out very well for us.) We have to get our noses in the Bible seek it out. As we've already read, the primary way to hear from God is through His word. When we do find out what God has to say about it, then we can start applying our faith.

There are some things in scripture that are automatic. God is crystal clear in His word about certain things and His will for us to have them. In 2 Peter 3:9, Peter writes, *"The Lord is not slack concerning His promise, as some count slackness, but is longsuffering toward us, not willing that any should perish but that all should come to repentance."* The Master doesn't want to see anyone permanently separated from Him for eternity. It is absolutely God's will for us to be saved. We shouldn't ever doubt this free gift of salvation!

Healing falls in this same category. David writes in Psalms 103:2-4, *"Bless the Lord, O my soul, and forget not all His benefits: Who forgives all your iniquities, who heals all your diseases, who redeems your life from destruction, who crowns you with loving kindness and tender mercies."* To further prove this point, Peter wrote in his first letter 2:24, *"who Himself bore our sins in His own body on the tree, that we, having died to sins, might live for righteousness—by whose stripes you were healed.*" Centuries of religious tradition have tried to snuff this simple truth out, but as Christians we aren't called to follow religion, we are called to follow Jesus and His word. Healing IS God's will. I'm sure I will get some nasty emails about this, but I didn't make it up; it's in the Bible and it is truth.

Provision and having our physical needs met is also God's perfect will. No one is getting blessed by us being broke or homeless. Many people would have us believe that we need to be free from material possessions to focus on God, but this runs in direct opposition to scripture. In Matthew 6:31-32, the author writes, *"Therefore do not worry, saying, 'What shall we eat?' or 'What shall we drink?' or 'What shall we wear?' For after all these things*

Gentiles seek. For your heavenly Father knows that you need all these things." And in Philippians 4:19, Paul writes, *"And my God shall supply all your need according to His riches in glory by Christ Jesus."* We are called to be God's hands and feet in this world, but it's hard to be a blessing to others if we don't have enough to cover our own bills. This is not what our good Father wants for His kids. I could give out another two dozen scriptures saying the same thing. God wants us to be blessed so we can be a blessing. I'll get more hate because of this paragraph than the last one, but I won't back down from what I know to be true!

Of course salvation, healing, and provision aren't the only automatics of God's will. He is a God who desires His people to have peace. Psalms 29:11 reads, *"The Lord will give strength to His people; the Lord will bless His people with peace."* He is a God who desires to see His people set free from any bondage or addiction. Paul writes in Galatians 5:1, *"Stand fast therefore in the liberty by which Christ has made us free, and do not be entangled again with a yoke of bondage."* And God desires justice for His children. Isaiah 61:8-9 reads, *"For I, the Lord, love justice; I hate robbery for burnt offering; I will direct their work in truth, and will make with them an everlasting covenant. Their descendants shall be known among the Gentiles, and their offspring among the people. All who see them shall acknowledge them, that they are the posterity whom the Lord has blessed."* These are the benefits of living in faith! The Psalmist talked about it in Psalms 103 that we read earlier. He is a good Father that wants good things for His kids.

Wow, so if all these things are God's will, then why don't we already have them? Everybody should be healthy, wealthy, saved and free; basically living in a perfect world. If it's the Father's good pleasure to bless us, then why aren't we all living in nirvana? The short answer is simply this: free will. There would be no reason to use faith if our lives were already perfect. We would be robots. The things that define us in our Christian life are the choices we make. Jesus isn't going to *invade* anyone's life. God isn't going to impose His will on everyone just because He can. He wants us to choose Him, and choose doing things His way. We have to ask God to be our Master and Savior and by faith we believe that He accepts us. That's how our Christian life begins and it is the same way our Christian life is lived: by faith. We have to choose to honor God and follow His commandments. In the gospel account of John chapter 14:15, Jesus says, *"If you love Me, keep My commandments."* My wife and I choose to honor God with our finances by tithing and giving. We do this because God commands it, but we also do it by faith knowing that as we honor God, He will in turn, honor us. The author of First Samuel writes in chapter 2 verse 30, *"Therefore the Lord God of Israel* says: 'I said indeed that your house and the house of your father would walk before Me forever.' But now the Lord says: 'far be it from Me; for those who honor Me I will honor, and those who despise Me shall be lightly esteemed.'" Keeping His commandments will always put us in a place of honor in God's eyes. As we read earlier, one of His commandments is for us to have faith to please Him. And to truly have faith, we have to know His will, and to know His will we must hear from Him.

Stay in your place

The second fundamental of faith is this; stay in your place. While the first rule may be the most commonly broken, the breaking of rule #2 isn't rare either. As is the case with any precept of biblical living, our flesh (human nature) is our greatest threat to this rule. We as human beings are not the most patient creatures alive. We live in a text message, microwave, drive-thru, Snapchat kind of society today. We don't like to wait (present company included). While this may be part of our nature, it isn't the way God created us to be. This impatient tendency has created a host of problems for our generation. Healthy eating habits? So much dust in the wind. Investing in a savings plan? Ugh, it takes too long to accrue. Wait until I get to my destination to text someone? Nah, I got this bro (insert crash sound here).

Watch a commercial? Ain't nobody got time fo' that! That's why I have a DVR! Actually getting to know someone before jumping into a relationship? Gone the way of the dinosaur.

This lack of patience is even more devastating for our spiritual lives than for our physical ones. Hearing from God is wonderful and exciting, whether learning something from His word or hearing from Him in a more personal way. However, God rarely gives us a timeline for His promises. If He did everything immediately, there would be little need for faith at all. Sometimes God simply wants to see if we will hang on to His promises, even if everything we see points in a different direction. In the Old Testament book of Habakkuk, chapter 3 and verses 17 through 19 the author writes, *"Though the fig tree may not blossom, nor fruit be on the vines; Though the labor of the olive may fail, and the fields yield no food; Though the flock may be cut off from the fold, and there be no herd in the stalls—Yet I will rejoice in the Lord, I will joy in the God of my salvation. The Lord God is my strength; He will make my feel like deer's feet, and He will make me walk on my high hills."* The prophet knew that no matter how dire circumstances looked, God would bring his people out on top. A clearer example of this is written in James 1:2-4. It reads, *"My brethren, count it all joy when you fall into various trials, knowing that the testing of your faith produces patience. But let patience have its perfect work, that you may be perfect and complete, lacking nothing.*" Our promise from God may not come right away, but we cannot give up on it. Patience is more than a virtue. It is a measuring stick of our faith. In fact, you could say that we don't have any more faith than we have patience.

What does this mean in real world application? Simply this: don't get out of your place. This refers to geographically, spiritually and even emotionally. If God has us planted somewhere: STAY THERE! We discussed earlier that He has a specific place in His kingdom for us. If we are where God led us, then we don't need to be leaving until He gives us the green light to do so. This is one of the most common mistakes I see among *church folk*. Usually the catalyst is a particularly well preached sermon that stepped on a few toes, or possibly a church congregation member that does us wrong (at least in our humble opinion), and all of a sudden we are looking for a new church. I know that I have been the victim of the church rumor-mill a time or ten (sometimes guilty of the rumor, sometimes not). There have been times that I have been so upset with a situation at church that I wanted to pack up my toys and go. I have seen people ostracized so completely because of a simple mistake or lapse in judgment that they went off the grid and were never seen by anyone in that church again. If you get put into this situation, what is the proper course of action? Did someone do you wrong? Maybe. Did people judge you unfairly? Maybe. Is it okay to feel hurt? Absolutely. Is it okay to request a scenery change? Sure. Is it okay to react immediately? Usually not. Can you put on your boogie shoes and beat it? No!

If you have been putting a sincere effort forth to be led by God, and you know that God led you to your present location, then only He can move you somewhere else. Well.... I mean you can move yourself, but if you get out of your place, you will be a miserable soul. This goes equally for staying put when God is calling us elsewhere. I can testify to that! The church I attended before my present church was and is a great place. I had been out of church for a decade or so and I had been running from God and His calling on my life for a long time. I had quite a few family members that went to this church so I started attending. That first year was a breath of fresh air to my spirit. I renewed my on-again off-again relationship with God, and He caused a maturing in me that can only be described as supernatural. It felt like every sermon was just for me. I received countless revelations as I read the Bible. I knew without a doubt that I was where I was supposed to be. After a couple of years however, I felt like God was calling me to move along. Was there a blow-up? Not at all. Did I get offended? On the contrary, I didn't want to go anywhere else. I brushed off that tug on my spirit and wrote it off as the enemy trying to get me out of my place. Do you see how important it is to stay sensitive to the Holy Spirit? I was giving the enemy credit for what God wanted to do with me.

My spiritual growth hit a plateau as did my service in the church. I still served on the worship team and was faithful in attendance and service, but I no longer felt fulfilled. In Isaiah 1:19 the author writes, "*If you are willing and obedient, you shall eat the good of the land; But if you refuse and rebel, You shall be devoured by the sword'; For the mouth of the Lord has spoken.*" Now I wasn't being chased by anyone with a scimitar, but I was definitely not being willing and obedient to His voice. There are always consequences following disobedience. Yes, God is patient and will put up with our "stanky attitude" and stubbornness longer than any human is capable, but He will send us reminders (in increasing levels of discomfort) to get us back on track. Mine started off with a plateau in my spiritual maturity and ended with being miserable.

At first I was confused over my stagnation, but eventually I got the hint. I would love to say that I jumped into action right then, but that would be a lie. I continued to rebel against the growing knowledge that I wasn't where I was supposed to be. I began a dating relationship with a girl in the church and that further hardened my resolve to stick it out right where I was. The relationship eventually failed, probably as a result of my stubbornness as much as anything else. Things in my family life had taken a nosedive. I felt spiritually dry, and now I was dealing with heartbreak. Well, that was finally enough to get me moving. I went and talked to my pastor and explained what was going on. Thankfully he is a man of character that is certainly Spirit led. He not only understood my plight, but told me to scoot along and not delay. That may sound harsh, but it wasn't at all. He understood the danger of being in the wrong place and how that can affect not only me, but any ministry in which I was involved. I still hold him in high respect and value his friendship to this day.

I began doing church visits the following Sunday and I spent a month attending different houses of worship and praying for clarity and wisdom. Going to church is important to me but finding where God wants me is just as important. After a month of visiting, I felt a peace about Southern Illinois Worship Center. I sensed God giving me the green light and after sitting through a few months of services, I went through the membership process and got involved. Having attended smaller churches all of my life; SIWC was a little intimidating at first. It was one of the largest churches in the area and although I knew a few people who called it home, I didn't know many people. However, within a few months, I was approached about joining the worship team and I was off and running. My family life had stabilized; I felt the spiritual maturation process pick up where it had left off; and while attending a marriage class, I met my future wife.

How did everything come together so quick? I was willing and obedient to God's will. While it is a fundamental truth that everything we receive is due to God's grace and not by our works, it is just as true that God rewards obedience! In Romans 2:6-8 Paul writes, "*who 'will render to each one according to his deeds': eternal life to those who by patient continuance in doing good seek for glory, honor, and immortality; but to those who are self-seeking and do not obey the truth, but obey unrighteousness—indignation and wrath,*."Find your place! Stay in your place!

Speak life

The third fundamental of faith is just as vital and powerful as the first two, but it is far and away, the most maligned and verbally abused. And as crazy as it may sound, this faith precept is ridiculed by just as many believers as non-believers. When discussing this subject it leaves a bad taste in the mouths of a lot of people. Many people would dance around this area of faith for fear of offending or being *labeled*. It is too vital of a subject for me to skip or gloss over however, so I will meet it head on and with scripture to back it! The reason I am so vehement about speaking life is because I have seen firsthand what the other end of speaking life looks like. If I can lay the groundwork for this subject in any way, it would be like this; there are two realities. There is the reality that we can experience with our five senses. What we see, what we hear, etc. Then there is the reality of what the word of God tells us. You have to choose which reality is going to define you and your walk with God. Those who live by their senses see this other reality as delusion or simply as lying (and they aren't afraid to tell you that....loudly....angrily.... and repetitively). However, those of us who live by the reality of what God's word says, are simply coming into agreement with Him.

Already there are people who have just put this book down and won't open it back up. I have never seen the amount of venom that come from believers when talking about speaking life. Now granted, there are people who try to misuse the whole idea. We can fall off the beam on either side and we are equally wrong, but agreeing with God's word will never steer us wrong. If I'm sick, I am not denying that I am sick, but as we read earlier in I Peter "*by His stripes we are healed.*" Therefore I am calling myself healed. It isn't any different than saying that our sins have been forgiven and we are saved. There is no outward proof of this, but that's what the bible says; so by faith we believe in our heart and confess with our mouth. Paul writes in Philippians 4:19, "*And my God shall supply all your need according to His riches in glory by Christ Jesus.*" Therefore, if I am having financial troubles I simply agree with the God-breathed word and call all of my needs met. There is no fine line, or semantics involved; it is simply agreeing with the word. God's reality is more real to me than what my senses tell me. In other words, I refuse to contradict what God's word says about my life and purpose.

The Bible is pretty specific about the power of our words for good or for ill. When you think about it, God created this universe and everything in it with His words and we were created in His image! God has always intended us to use our words as implements of power. Let's look at some scripture having to do with the importance and power of our tongue. James really goes into detail about how powerful and unruly our tongue is. James 3:3-12 reads, "*Indeed, we put bits in horses' mouths that they may obey us, and we turn their whole body. Look also at ships: although they are so large and are driven by fierce winds, they are turned by a very small rudder wherever the pilot desires. Even so the tongue is a little member and boasts great things. See how great a forest a little fire kindles! And the tongue is a fire, a world of iniquity. The tongue is so set among our members that it defiles the whole body, and sets on fire the course of nature; and it is set on fire by hell. For every kind of beast and bird, of reptile and creature of the sea, is tamed and has been tamed by mankind. But no man can tame the tongue. It is an unruly evil, full of deadly poison. With it we bless our God and Father, and with it we curse men, who have been made in the similitude of God. Out of the same mouth proceed blessing and cursing. My brethren, these things ought not to be so. Does a spring send forth fresh water and bitter from the same opening? Can a fig tree, my brethren, bear olives, or a grapevine bear figs? Thus no spring yields both salt water and fresh."*

Lengthy passage, I know, but I think it really stresses the authority and nature of our words. Proverbs 18:21 reads, "*Death and life are in the power of the tongue, and those who love it will eat its fruit.*"Life and death??! Believe me, I wouldn't be spending so much time on this subject if it wasn't so significant. Jesus demonstrated the power of words during His earthly ministry, but He also gave us directions on how to use our words as well. Mark 11:22-23 reads, "So Jesus *answered and said to them, "Have faith in God. For assuredly, I say to you, whoever **says** to this mountain, 'Be removed and be cast into the sea,' and does not doubt in his heart, but believes that those things he **says** will be done, he will have whatever he **says**."* (Emphasis added by me) Jesus doesn't say that whoever wants the mountain moved, or whoever thinks about the mountain being moved, but whoever says to the mountain. Jesus spoke to fig trees, spoke to fevers, and spoke to wind and waves as well. Since He is our model, we need to emulate Him. Jesus knew the power of words and how they affected the heavens.

Speaking life is crucial to your faith growth, but the other main reason this section is so necessary is the other end of the spectrum; what I call dyslexic faith. Dyslexic faith is using your words, whether purposefully or unintentional, to speak negativity. We've all experienced this to some degree. Children are notorious for saying cruel or demeaning things to each other. Unfortunately kids don't hold the patent on negative words. Many adults speak to their kids or spouses in insults and criticisms causing not only damage to their self-esteem, but teaching them to speak to others the same way.

This has come under the magnifying glass to a much greater degree in the last ten years because of the Internet, social media, and awareness campaigns about bullying. It has become obvious that while dyslexic faith is certainly a spiritual issue, even non-believers know the power of negativity and how that can affect people. The real problem behind the destructive nature of people's language and harsh words is the condition of their heart. I'm not talking about the organ that pumps blood, but the core of who someone really is: the essence of one's emotional, moral, and intellectual self. In the gospel account of Luke, Jesus says in chapter 6 verse 45, "*A good man out of the good treasure of his heart brings forth good; and an evil man out of the evil treasure of his heart brings forth evil. For out of the abundance of the heart his mouth speaks.*" What is in your heart will come out of your mouth!

Now before anyone gets all bent out of shape about this, let me be clear; I'm not suggesting that negative confessions are spiritual voodoo dolls. Every little kid playing "step on a crack and break your mother's back" isn't causing their parental unit spinal issues. When someone says, "I'm dying of thirst," the chances of them expiring from dehydration are slim to none. The very idea of this is, understandably, ludicrous. God isn't some cosmic cop with his finger on a hair trigger waiting for you to say something sarcastic so He can jump on you.

However, as we have firmly established through scripture, our words are powerful. As Jesus said in Luke, what is in our heart will come out our mouth. If we are constantly talking negative about others or ourselves, there is a danger that we have established "faith" about what we are saying;

and this is not the kind of faith you want! Let me clarify with more scripture. James in Chapter 1 verse 26 writes in his letter, "*If anyone among you thinks he is religious, and does not bridle his tongue but deceives his own heart, this one's religion is useless.*" Ecclesiastes 10:12 reads, "*The words of a wise man's mouth are gracious, but the lips of a fool shall swallow him up.*" Proverbs 11:9 declares, "*The hypocrite with his mouth destroys his neighbor, but through knowledge the righteous will be delivered.*" Faith is wonderful and gives our heavenly Father something tangible to work with in our lives, but faith works in both directions. If we honestly believe the lies that the enemy tells us and we confess those lies constantly, we are using our faith in a way that God never intended.

My cousin "Jack" and his wife "Debbie" (I have changed their names for privacy's sake) have some acquaintances at their church that are prime examples of what I'm talking about. This family has been on the prayer request list every week for six years running. My cousin said that he had never seen a run of bad luck like what this family has been through. I won't go into details, so as to protect their identity, but an outside observer might think that God has forsaken these people. They served in the church. They were faithful. They love God and people. What could possibly be the problem? According to Jack, one thirty minute conversation with them would spell it out quite clearly. They firmly believe that the worst will always happen to them. They are constantly waiting for the other shoe to drop. Jack and Debbie tried for over a year to speak life and faith to them. This family would always come to them with their problems and they would try our best to encourage them. Actually, God helped Jack and Debbie develop quite a marriage and family ministry during this time. God was giving them all the right things to say and this couple was nodding and agreeing in all the right places, but after each conversation, they knew; these parents weren't getting it. They were only looking for commiseration. After a dozen or more of these intense counseling sessions, Debbie and Jack both felt that this couple was pulling them down instead of them pulling the family up. They felt led to distance themselves from the situation a bit. They obeyed, but they were both frustrated that they weren't able to help them more.

Not too long after hearing this account from my cousin, I was reading in my morning devotional time and God led me to Mark chapter 6 verses 3 through 6. Jesus and His disciples are just leaving Jesus' hometown and the author writes, " *'Is this not the carpenter, the Son of Mary, and brother of James, Joses, Judas, and Simon? And are not His sisters here with us?' So they were offended at Him. But Jesus said to them, 'A prophet is not without honor except in his own country, among his own relatives, and in his own* *house.' Now He **could** do no mighty work there, except that He laid His hands on a few sick people and healed them. And He marveled because of their unbelief. Then He went about the villages in a circuit, teaching."* (Emphasis mine) Jesus was the son of God, right? Surely He just chose to do no mighty work there, right? That isn't what the infallible word of God says. It says He couldn't do any mighty work there. Why not? It tells you in the next verse - their unbelief. This family that my cousin and his wife had been counseling believed that God was capable of delivering them from their circumstances, but not that He was willing to do so. They were using the salvation concept, but in a perverted way. They believed that bad things were going to happen and they were confessing with their mouths that bad things were going to happen. Job said it pretty accurately in the Old Testament. Job 3:25 reads *"For the thing I greatly feared has come upon me, and what I dreaded has happened to me."* Dyslexic faith.

Already I am preparing my email inbox for the flood of outraged Christians telling me that God has a sense of humor, that God knows when they are just kidding around, or that they don't really mean anything by what they're saying. Well, I'm glad you mentioned that because Jesus addressed this type of talk as well. Matthew writes in his gospel account in chapter 12 verses 36-37, *"But I say to you that for every idle word men may speak, they* will give account of it in the day of judgment. For by your words you will be justified, and by your words you will be condemned." So what is an idle word? The Greek word translated idle in this verse is the word argos. This word literally means *inactive* or *useless*. Words have power and are meant to have power. Powerless words or *idle talk* will have consequences of their own. Of course the best way to back up scripture is with more scripture! Proverbs 17:27 reads, "*He who has knowledge spares his words, and a man of understanding is of a calm spirit.*" Proverbs 13:3 declares, "*He who guards his mouth preserves his life, but he who opens wide his lips shall have destruction.*" Perhaps most direct is Proverbs 10:19. It says, "*In the multitude of words sin is not lacking, but he who restrains his lips is wise.*" We may not mean anything by the words we speak, but if negative confessions become a ritual or habit there is danger ahead! Choosing our words carefully and being slow to sound off are good pieces of advice for any Christian. And never let your faith work against you. Speak life!

Chapter 4

<u>You Be Trippin' !!!</u>

Sin: Mirage or Menace? Story at 11!

The gravitationally challenged letter carrier was trying to replace the person-hole cover in the street while three vertically challenged gender neutral nonbinary citizens constructed a snow-person. *sigh* Welcome to the 21st century. I am not saying that all politically correct language is wrong. There were some terms and labels that were commonly used while I was growing up that were just plain cruel or wrong. I get it. However, we as a generation have been responsible for using political correctness as a substitution for honesty and common sense. We no longer have elderly people, we have the gerentologically advanced. No one is poor, they are economically unprepared. Is he rude? Nope, he is charismatically impeded. Did you have a loved one pass away? They aren't dead, they are living impaired. These PC ideals that we have fostered in the effort to not offend have created a culture that is needlessly touchy and ultrasensitive. To the torch bearers of this PC movement, even specifying someone's God-given gender triggers an automatic outrage. I was told about a professor who once told a group of college students to "keep their minds open—but not so open that your brains fall out." Aaaaaannnnd... here we are.

I would love to say that at least the church has stayed immune to the PC culture, but I can't. Instead of the church shaping our culture, our culture has shaped the modern church. Corporate greed has driven many churches into the ground as funds are misused for lavish living. Social media has given people an outlet to propel the inevitable church rumor mill and transform it into ignorance or even focused hatred. The divorce rate in the church is identical to that of non-believers. However, the most glaring problem facing the culture of the church is simply a refusal to acknowledge sin. Just saying the word makes both Christians and non-believers squirm. In today's society, we prefer the word "issues."

We know that Johnny likes to get hammered on whiskey and tune up on his wife's face, but it's an "issue" and he is working on it. Huh??! It's not an issue, it's not a weakness, it is sin! "Feel good sermons" may help to fill up a church (temporarily at least), but to become a mature Christian we need to acknowledge that there is an enemy. We must recognize that the enemy will try to get us to violate our conscience and what we know is right. And we must admit that sin is real, it will mess up our life. To repent means to change our direction. These are some of the basic building blocks for a Christian life and we can't ignore them. Grace is wonderful and God's goodness should be touted at all times, but not at the expense of the full truth. Sin is real and there are real consequences for breaking the laws of God!

Merriam-Webster defines sin this way: an offense against religious or moral law, or a transgression of the law of God. I guess in some ways these dictionary definitions are accurate, but there is a bit more to it. Sin is really a violation of our conscience. It is choosing to go against what we know is right. When you first begin our new life as a Christian, you aren't going to know much. Many aspects of your day-to-day life will continue on as it always has, for better or for worse. There may be parts of your lifestyle that don't line up with God's law and His desire for His people, but you won't know all of this right away. As you mature in your relationship with God, He will illuminate more and more areas of your life that need to be changed. As you receive this illumination, you are now responsible for that knowledge. Sin is really just a refusal to acknowledge what you know is right or wrong.

I worked as a restaurant server for almost eighteen years of my life spanning my twenties and most of my thirties. It was good money for someone with no degree and who lived a single lifestyle. In both of the restaurants in which I worked, we did not have to turn in our tips. We only had to claim how much we made for tax purposes. No one that I was aware of claimed everything that they made. The general consensus was that claiming eight to ten percent of your total sales for the shift was enough to keep from being audited. A few servers even claimed as high as fifteen percent. I was a twelve percent kind of guy. Because it was the normal procedure, I never felt one bit of guilt about this. Many times twelve percent was pretty close to accurate, especially in the first few years of serving. However, as I got better at my job and established regular customers, I was always clearing fifteen to twenty percent of my sales. Still, I felt no guilt or condemnation for claiming less because everyone else did as well. For goodness sake, I claimed a higher percentage than most people so I even felt morally superior.

Eventually, God started dealing with my heart and I got back into church and turned my life over to Him. Not too much changed in my life right away. My serving career marched on unchanged for over a year. However, one day in a time of prayer, God questioned my integrity when it came to my tip claiming process. I was indignant at first. I argued that I claimed more than anyone else did and that should count for something! As this heated one-sided discussion continued, I began to realize that "only being a little dishonest" was a pretty sorry excuse for cheating the government out of taxes. My character was on the line and any one of my co-workers who knew that I didn't claim all of my income would feel justified in doing the same. I had to repent and to change the way I did my job.

I can honestly say that I had never put the concepts of "claiming a lower percentage" and "cheating on my taxes" together until that moment. I had been doing it that way for twelve or thirteen years because that's how everyone did it. So did I wallow in guilt for the past decade of being dishonest? I really didn't. In the book of John, Jesus has just healed a blind man and the Pharisees (religious folks) had kicked the man out of the temple accusing him of giving Jesus too much credit. Jesus finds the man and reveals Himself to the man as the Son of God. The man believes and worships Jesus. John 9:39-41 reads, "*And Jesus said, 'For judgment I have come into this world, that those who do not see may see, and that those who see may be made blind.' Then some of the Pharisees who were with Him heard these words, and said to Him, 'Are we blind also?' Jesus said to them, 'If you were blind, you would have no sin; but now you say, 'We see.' Therefore your sin remains.'*"

God doesn't hold you accountable for what you don't see. This doesn't mean that there are no consequences for your actions, only that He doesn't count it against you as sin. The law of gravity still works whether you know about it or not. If you jump from a high place, you're going to land hard. If you accidentally walk in front of a moving vehicle, you're probably going to have a pretty bad day. However, God does not hold you responsible for what you don't know. In Romans 5:13 Paul writes, "*For until the law sin was in the world, but sin is not imputed when there is no law.*" I had been cheating the government for a long time by claiming less than I should have been but I was ignorant of any wrongdoing. When God showed me how I was being dishonest, I had a choice to make. I could continue to violate what I now knew was the right thing to do (commit sin). Or I could change my ways and start to do things the right way (true repentance). I made the right decision and was rewarded with four or five of the most monetarily lucrative years of serving that I had ever experienced. This is not to say that walking away from sinful behavior is a "blessing slot machine." Repent, pull the lever and profit!! It doesn't work that way, but there are most certainly rewards for being obedient and doing things God's way!

I live therefore I sin… (but I don't live in sin)

One of the big temptations for new Christians, especially after they learn about the grace of God and the redemptive and cleansing power of Jesus' blood, is to use God's mercy and forgiveness as a license for doing whatever they feel like. As I've mentioned before, I was raised in a religious culture that stressed judgment over grace. I remember many times spent begging for forgiveness at the church altar. I would cry, plead, and generally debase myself until I felt I had earned God's mercy. I recall thinking, "I hope God takes me right now because I'm clean. If he waits another hour or two, I will undoubtedly mess up and then I'm doomed." This mentality of never being good enough would do one of two things: make you stay "super holy" (leaving you feeling paranoid and miserable) or make you leave the church because you feel you can't measure up (leaving you feeling convicted and miserable). Neither option was satisfying. Grace was considered by some a dirty word unless it was preceded by "Amazing" and was sang from the hymnal.

This may sound like I'm bitter about my upbringing and spiritual heritage, but I'm really not. Yes, there were some gaping holes in the theology, but I received a foundation in the works of the Holy Spirit and spiritual gifts that I could not have received in any other denomination where I lived at that time. No branch of Christianity has it all correct, and we should never assume we know better than the other guy. I am thankful and appreciative of my heritage and the dedicated church elders that served as my role models growing up. Regardless, mercy was not a subject often taught. Forgiveness was to be earned by the sweat of your brow and the works of your hand.

Then I began to study the Bible and I got my hands on some teaching about the power of God's grace. Have you ever heard the idiom of "knowing just enough to be dangerous"? Well, that described me pretty accurately. I was able to blithely jump from the ditch on one side of the road to the ditch on the opposite side. I let things into my life that had no business being there, "but hey, God's mercies are new every morning." That's Bible, folks! It really irritated me that I still had to deal with my conscience though. The attitudes, actions, and speech that I had adopted in my new found "liberty" still bothered me a bit. However, I found that by cutting my prayer time by eighty percent and not attending church as regularly, my conscience's voice was much quieter. I would ask for forgiveness for doing something I knew wasn't right, knowing full well that I had plans to do it again that weekend. Within a short time, I wasn't even pretending to live for God anymore. I used God's grace and mercy as a license for sin.

Some may ask, isn't that what mercy and grace is there for? I am so glad you asked! In the early days of the church, many people asked the same questions. In the Apostle Paul's letter to the Romans, he addressed these concerns being voiced by the church. Chapter 6 verse 1 reads, "*What shall we say then? Shall we continue in sin, that grace may abound? Certainly not! How shall we, who died to sin, live any longer in it?*" Verses 14-16 continue in much the same vein as Paul writes, "*For sin shall not have dominion over you, for you are not under law but under grace. What then? Shall we sin because we are not under law but under grace? Certainly not! Do you not know that to whom you present yourselves slaves to obey, you are that one's slaves whom you obey, whether of sin leading to death, or of obedience leading to righteousness.*"

I had learned just enough to know that the blood of Jesus would cover any sin, no matter what it was. I learned that God would never turn His back on me. However, I decided that I could use that knowledge to live however I pleased. As Paul points out, that is not at all how it works. In Galatians chapter 5 and verse 13, Paul writes, "*For you, brethren, have been* called to liberty; only do not use liberty as an opportunity for the flesh, but through love serve one another." In verse 24 of the same chapter he writes, "And those who are Christ's have crucified the flesh with its passions and desires." The Apostle Paul was crystal clear that a true follower of Jesus would never use the grace and freedom that we have through Christ as a license to sin. Jesus Himself said, "If you love Me, keep my commandments." (John 14:15) If we can't be obedient to God's commandments, then our love and dedication for Jesus is called into question. The author of Hebrews writes in chapter 10 and verse 26, "For if we sin willfully after we have received the knowledge of the truth, there no longer remains a sacrifice for sins." That's some pretty strong language isn't it?

Does this mean we have to be perfect?!! It certainly means we should strive to be as much like Jesus as possible, but He is the only one who has lived a perfect life. The Bible mentions working toward perfection several times. In Matthew chapter 5 and verse 48, he writes, "Therefore you shall be perfect, just as your Father in heaven is perfect." The author writes in Deuteronomy 18:13, "You shall be blameless before the Lord your God." But to understand these references, we must realize that the Greek work translated perfect does NOT mean flawless or devoid of sin. It simply means complete, mature, or fully grown. As we've discovered already, God expects us to grow up. Part of the maturation process of a Christian is bringing our wants and desires into line with God's. He lets us know His will for us in His holy word. In II Timothy 3:16-17, Paul says, "*All scripture is given by inspiration of God, and is profitable for doctrine, for reproof, for correction , for instruction in righteousness, that the man of God may be complete, thoroughly equipped for every good work.*" The word complete in this verse is a companion word for the Greek word for perfect. Flawless may be unattainable, but whole and complete are definitely within reach!

Continue from latest save point

I'm not a gamer. I just want to make that abundantly clear. Please don't send me emails about my lack of gaming knowledge. My video game info comes primarily from my kids. I am not one of those people who think video games are gateways to the Underworld. My wife and I buy the occasional Madden or NBA Live game for the boys at Christmas, but video game-time is rationed. That being said, I was a teenager once too, and I remember playing games on my 8-bit original Nintendo console. Some of my favorite games were adventure games that involved solving puzzles and defeating enemy bosses to advance to the next level. The one thing that would make me lose my temper quicker than anything else was when my character would die and I had forgotten to save my progress. A few of these evil, twisted, maniacal, and overall devilish games would make you start at the very beginning when your character died. What kind of warped mind would make a game like this??! After a couple of times of getting burned, I learned to save my progress -a lot. In fact I saved every couple of minutes. I saved so often that I would forget and save on top of another save. Then I would save again just to be sure.

As I've mentioned, my religious upbringing was rather strict. When it came to dealing with sin, it was much like the Nintendo games with no save points. When you screwed up, and you always would, then you would go all the way back to the beginning; and let me tell you, it was always a long walk back. I was taught (or at least led to believe) that any and all sin would take you back to non-believer status. As I write this now, I realize that not everyone around me really believed that way, but it was certainly the way we portrayed it, intentionally or not. Members of the congregation were always trying to spread the Gospel and lead people to Jesus, but the church never grew. Many times I saw good Christian people simply stop attending church, and often they would revert to a lifestyle that was more outrageous than anything they did before becoming a believer. As I got older (and more rebellious), I began to understand and sympathize with these people. I mean really, why bother? There is no way I could live up to God's standard anyway. Satan had me convinced that my Christianity was like a tightrope walk. Every time I would fall (sin), I would get back on my feet (after wallowing in guilt for a few days of course) and I would head back to the ladder (the altar) to start the climb back up to the rope so I could start my balancing act again. Eventually, I got sick of the "walk of shame" back to the ladder to start over, so I quit.

For close to 20 years I was out of the church and running from God. One night after a card game with some acquaintances, a friend, who knew I was having a tough time, gave me a set of sermons on CD. I had never been one to listen to taped preaching, but it gave me something to listen to on my commute to work. I hadn't realized how hungry my spirit was for the Word of God! I started obtaining more and more preaching and teaching CDs. I started attending church again regularly, and I received some pretty mind blowing revelations. One of the biggest and most life-altering realizations was that Christian living was not a tightrope; it was a sidewalk. It was like a video game that auto-saved every 2 or 3 minutes. When I fell, there was no walk of shame. It was simply standing back up! Of course, there were the natural consequences of my actions to deal with, but spiritually I was still in the same place that I was when I fell! It took several months before I was able to fully accept this idea. Naturally, when you fall or sin you must repent, but when God forgives you there is no losing ground. I didn't have to hit the reset button, or re-fight an enemy that I had already beaten. In the book of Isaiah chapter 43 and verse 25, the prophet is speaking the words of God saying, "*I, even I am He who blots out your transgressions for my own sake and remembers your sins no more.*" Once you are forgiven, God doesn't remember your sins and you don't need to dwell on them either!

I'm telling your Dad!!!!

So why was it so hard for me to accept this wonderful news about God's forgiveness and grace? It wasn't simply my upbringing. In Psalms 38:17-18 the psalmist writes, "*For I will declare my iniquity; I will be in anguish over my sin.*" In Psalms 40:12 David says, "*For innumerable evils have surrounded me; My iniquities have overtaken me, so that I am not able to look up; Therefore my heart fails me.*" According to scripture (Acts 13:22), David was a man after God's own heart, yet he wrote both of these Psalms crying out to God because he felt the weight of his sin. If God forgives us, then why do we feel the guilt? The answer lies in Revelation chapter 12 and verse 10. John writes, "*Then I heard a loud voice saying in heaven, 'Now salvation, and strength, and the kingdom of our God, and the power of His*

Christ have come, for the accuser of our brethren, who accused them before our God day and night, has been cast down." The enemy of our souls stands accusing us day and night before the throne of God. And he makes quite certain that you are able to hear him when he does it. Satan will go to great lengths to remind you of every time you have messed up. He delights in helping you remember how many people you have hurt, how many times you disgraced yourself, and how you are still the same old person you always were. However, God gave us a way to battle the enemy -- the Word of God. Paul writes in Romans 8:1 "*There is therefore now no condemnation to those who are in Christ Jesus, who do not walk according to the flesh, but according to the Spirit.*" That tells us where the guilt and condemnation DON'T come from. God will convict, but never use guilt. Shame and guilt are devices of Satan, not God.

So how do we know the difference between condemnation and conviction? It's actually a rather simple distinction. While conviction and condemnation will both illuminate things in our life that need to be changed, guilt will make us want to get farther away from God to hide our action or inaction, while conviction will drive us closer to the Father. Conviction inspires us to change and strive for improvement. Guilt will always try to conceal and cover up sin and will encourage us to keep anything having to do with God at a distance. In all of my experience, guilt is the single biggest factor that drives people from church and from God. I know it kept **me** away for over two decades. In II Corinthians 7:10 Paul explains, "*For Godly sorrow produces repentance leading to salvation, not to be regretted; but the sorrow of the world produces death.*" Godly sorrow (conviction from the Holy Spirit) always produces a change while shame or guilt produces destruction.

This is not a new concept. From the beginning of time, Satan has used condemnation to drive a wedge between us and God. Genesis records the enemy's first interaction with humans. Satan came to Eve in the form of a serpent and persuaded her that God was holding back on her and Adam. They both disobeyed God's command not to eat of the forbidden tree. In Genesis 3:8-10 the scriptures read, "*And they heard the sound of the Lord God walking in the garden in the cool of the day, and Adam and his wife hid themselves from the presence of the Lord God among the trees of the garden. Then the Lord God called to Adam and said to him, 'Where are you?' So he said, 'I heard Your voice in the garden, and I was afraid because I was naked; and I hid myself.*" Sin resulted in shame and an attempt to hide from God. Ugh... I can relate.

So how can we get victory over our enemy who stands before God and accuses us constantly? If we read verse 10 of Revelation again and add verse 11 to it, we get a view of the bigger picture. It reads, *"Then I heard a loud voice saying in heaven, 'Now salvation, and strength, and the kingdom of our God, and the power of His Christ have come, for the accuser of our brethren, who accused them before our God day and night, **has been cast down. And they overcame him by the blood of the Lamb and by the word of their testimony**, and they did not love their lives to the death"* (emphasis mine).The blood of Jesus is the obvious part of the solution and we'll talk more about that in a bit. He died to take away all sins and to make us spotless before God. However, we are also set free from guilt and shame by the word of our testimony.

James 5:16 reads, *"Confess your trespasses to one another, and pray for one another, that you may be healed."* Bringing your sins into the light is a Biblical prescription for healing. Naturally, you need to be selective to whom you are confessing things. There are many people, even in the church, who would use any such confession as ammunition against you. God doesn't hold your past against you, and you don't need nosy judgmental people doing it either! However, there is something powerful in having accountability partners. There are several scriptures that back that up.

Proverbs 25:12 says, "*Like an earring of gold and an ornament of fine gold is a wise rebuke to an obedient ear.*" In chapter 27 and verse 17 of the same book, it reads, "*As iron sharpens iron, so a man sharpens the countenance of his friend.*" Paul writes in Galatians 6:1-2, "*Brethren, if a man is overtaken in any trespass, you who are spiritual restore such a one in a spirit of gentleness, considering yourself lest you also be tempted. Bear one another's burdens, and so fulfill the law of Christ.*"

      A few years ago, I was having some difficulties in breaking free from a gambling problem. I was firmly entrenched in the church and was serving faithfully. However, I was seeing a serious drain on my finances, my prayer life, and my joy because of the poker machines. I had spent a good deal of time praying about this issue, but I felt like I was losing ground. In a time of reading my Bible, I came across the scripture I mentioned above in Galatians. I felt like God was really pressing me to obtain some accountability in my life. I sought out a Godly man that I was friends with and told him about my problem and asked if he would serve as my accountability partner. I would love to say that was the magic combination that delivered me instantly, but I did slip up a few times after that. The first time I even lied to him when he asked how I was doing with it. I felt miserable for two days until I called him and fessed up. He checked on me several times after that and even though it was embarrassing for me, I told him the truth and he prayed with me and encouraged me. He didn't berate me, insult me, or shame me. Within a fairly short period of a month or two, I was completely free from that addiction! Doing things God's way will always be vastly superior to trying to do it on your own.

The Red Sea that doesn't part

The story in Exodus about the people of Israel fleeing from their Egyptian bondage is a pretty exciting narrative. God performs many miracles and wonders to persuade the Pharaoh to let His people go, but Pharaoh would not. This resulted in ten plagues being visited upon Egypt starting with the water being turned to blood and culminating with the death of every firstborn in the land. It was finally too much for Pharaoh and he let the Israelites go; but after releasing them, he had yet another change of heart and gave chase to bring them back. With Pharaoh's army in pursuit and quickly approaching the Red Sea which would cut off their escape, the Israelites looked to Moses to ask God to perform yet another miracle. There on the banks of the sea, Moses prayed and God parted the Red Sea and His people crossed on dry land.

As great of a story as that is, I want to end this chapter talking about an even greater red sea story. This red sea isn't a body of water but the blood of Jesus. I have heard many unbelievers talk about Christians' preoccupation with the blood of Christ, and how it is morbid and disgusting; but in this case, what they don't know *can* hurt them. We have a reverence and awe for the blood of Jesus because of the power that it invokes.

Before the coming of Jesus, God's people had to sacrifice lambs every year and the blood of these sacrifices would push their sins forward one year. However, Jesus was born into this world to be the final spotless sinless lamb that would be sacrificed to cover the sins of the entire world, if they would believe in Him. The author of Hebrews writes in chapter 13 and verses 11 and 12, "*For the bodies of those animals, whose blood is brought into the sanctuary by the high priest for sin, are burned outside the camp. Therefore Jesus also, that He might sanctify the people with his own blood, suffered outside the gate.*" Ephesians 1:7 reads, "*In Him we have redemption through His blood, the forgiveness of sins, according to the riches of His grace.*" These scriptures give you a real insight why we talk about the blood so much. It is only through His blood that we are saved, sanctified, healed, and set free. It is everything to us! When instituting communion at the Last Supper in Matthew 26:28 , Jesus said, "*for this is My blood of the covenant, which is poured out for many for forgiveness of sins.*" One drop of the precious blood of Jesus is enough to cleanse the sins of the world!

You might say, "Yeah, but you don't know what all I have done." Well, you don't know how powerful the blood of Jesus is! In I John 1:6, John writes, "*But if we walk in the light as He is in the light, we have fellowship with one another, and the blood of Jesus Christ His Son cleanses us from all sin.*" Notice he said ALL sin. There is no tricky Greek or Hebrew translation for all. It means all. There is no sin that the blood of Jesus cannot cleanse. The only way the blood doesn't work is if you don't accept it. As with any other aspect of your Christian life, forgiveness requires faith. However, once you accept that forgiveness, God can no longer even see your former life of sin; all He sees is the blood of his Son. It is this "once and for all" blood sacrifice that truly frees us and gives us the liberty and ability to work in God's kingdom with a fervent abandon that can only come from a pure heart. Hebrews 9:13-14 reads, "*For if the blood of bulls and goats and the ashes of a heifer, sprinkling the unclean, sanctifies for the purifying of the flesh, how much more shall the blood of Christ, who through the eternal Spirit offered Himself without spot to God, cleanse your conscience from dead works to serve the living God?*"While God parted the Red Sea for the Israelites and allowed them to cross on dry ground, Jesus' blood will never be separated from us. It is truly the red sea that doesn't part.

Chapter 5

Christian FAQs

Why do bad things happen to good people?

I believe this is the most asked question among Christians and non-Christians alike. Unbelievers are quite often using this question and its lack of a satisfactory answer, as their case for not believing in God. Christians are stuck dealing with this question after unexpected deaths of family or friends, financial devastations, or similar tragedies. I know I have asked this question of God before; just as you probably have or will at some point in the future. Luke tells a story in his gospel account that had people questioning Jesus about this very thing. Luke 13: 1-5 says, *"There were present at that season some who told Him and the Galileans whose blood Pilate had mingled with their sacrifices. And Jesus answered and said to them, 'Do you suppose that these Galileans were worse sinners than all other Galileans, because they suffered such things? I tell you no; but unless you repent you will all likewise perish. Or those eighteen on whom the tower in Siloam fell and killed them, do you think that they were worse sinners than all other men who dwelt in Jerusalem? I tell you, no; but unless you repent you will all likewise perish."* Some people had come to Jesus telling him about a tragedy that had befallen some believers. Pilate had swept in and slaughtered a whole group of worshippers in the temple and their blood had mingled with the blood of the sacrifices. Jesus made it quite clear that these folks were not any worse than anyone else. He said that it is only the mercy of God that keeps things from happening to any one of us.

It may be difficult to swallow for some people, especially believers, but life happens. People controlled by wicked desires exist and try to advance their causes. The rain falls on the innocent as well as the guilty. There is an enemy of our soul out there in the world, and he will do all that he can to bring us to ruin. So do we have any protection from God? ABSOLUTELY! As I look back on my 20s and 30s, I am amazed that I am still alive, let alone writing a book for the glory of God. His mercy keeps and protects us at all times, but that doesn't mean difficult times won't come. God is indeed all good, all light, and in Him is no darkness, but if we never had any troubles, we would never need to use our faith. And as we have learned, without faith it is impossible to please God. God allows us opportunities to test our faith and our resolve. In fact, Jesus Himself said in John 16:33, "*These things have I spoken to you, that in Me you may have peace. In the world you will have tribulation; but be of good cheer, I have overcome the world.*"

Yes, troubles will come but we have been created to overcome! The rain may come down on the righteous and unrighteous alike, but those with the firm foundation will withstand the storm intact. Notice Jesus said to be of good cheer. Why would He tell us to be cheerful while suffering? Because joy is a powerful ally. Nehemiah 8:10 says, "Then he said to them, '*Go your way, eat the fat, drink the sweet, and send portions to those for whom nothing is prepared; for this day is holy to our Lord. Do not sorrow, for the joy of the Lord is your strength.*'" Our strength comes from His joy! The Apostle Paul also writes to the people of Rome about staying joyful in the midst of trouble. Romans 5: 3-5 reads, "*And not only that, but we also glory in tribulations, knowing that tribulation produces perseverance; and perseverance, character; and character, hope. Now hope does not disappoint, because the love of God has been poured out in our hearts by the Holy Spirit who was given to us.*" Unfortunately, we are forced to exist in a fallen world where Satan can certainly exert at least some degree of influence; but hope is never lost as long as we can persevere and rejoice even in our troubles.

Another primary reason for God's allowance of evil in our lives is for the glory that comes from the deliverance. This is illustrated clearly in the Gospel of John. Chapter 9 and verses 1-3 read, "*Now as Jesus passed by, He saw a man who was blind from birth. And His disciples asked Him, saying,*

'Rabbi, who sinned, this man or his parents, that he was born blind?' Jesus answered, 'Neither this man nor his parents sinned, but that the works of God should be revealed in him'." The disciples were thinking the same way a lot of us do; he or his parents must have done something wrong for this man to be born blind. Jesus clears this up in a hurry by explaining that this tragedy came about so God could be glorified. Is God glorified in sickness? Never. Is He glorified in poverty? Not for one instant. So where does God get the glory? It is in the deliverance from these conditions that His power and glory are truly seen. Do you think that this blind man, after being healed by Jesus, was upset because he had to go through troubles? I don't think so! He was a living testimony of the power and glory of God!

If we never had to go through any troubles or bad circumstances, then how could we help someone else going through the same thing? Someone seeing God bring us through the bad times and coming out on the other side victorious might be the encouragement they need to make it through another day. Our testimony could be the push they need to give their life over to God. While you can't let your past define you, the willingness to let your past be a landmark of God's mercy and goodness will not only affect others, but will help you stay victorious as well. Remember: we are made overcomers by the blood of the Lamb, and the word of our testimony. Everyone wins!

I'm a Christian now, why do I still want to sin?

To answer this question with a one word answer: flesh. I'm not talking about the five or six yards of skin covering your skeleton, but about your sinful nature. The New Testament talks about "the flesh" in many scriptures, but only a handful of them are talking about anything physical. Almost all of the references to "the flesh" are talking about the part of our human nature that is alienated from God and His ways. When we come to Jesus and accept Him as our Lord and Savior, our spirit is made new, but our flesh isn't! We are going to wake up the next day and our flesh is going to want to keep on doing what it's been doing all along. This can be very confusing for a new Christian, because, we are so full of love and excitement when coming to God. How can we possibly still want to sin?

Well, we're in good company. The Apostle Paul…you know, the guy who wrote two-thirds of the New Testament and started more churches than anyone in his time, talked about his struggles with this as well. When writing to the church in Rome, he writes in Chapter 7 and verses 18-19, "*For I know that in me (that is, in my flesh) nothing good dwells; for to will is present with me, but how to perform what is good I do not find. For the good that I will to do, I do not do; but the evil I will not to do, that I practice.*" In a nutshell, Paul is saying, "I know that my flesh is always up to no good, but I'm not sure how to deny it. I want to do good things but I somehow ending doing just the opposite." Later in the same chapter but in verse 24 he writes, "*O wretched man that I am! Who will deliver me from this body of death?*" Paul clearly realizes that his human nature will always be in contention with God's wishes and is always striving for destruction.

There are many Christians, even some misguided pastors, who will try their best to convince you that because sin is deplorable, if you still have these desires and longings, there is something wrong with you. That is simply not true. Even the Bible admits that sin does come with pleasure. The author of Hebrews writes in chapter 11 and verses 24 and 25, "*By faith Moses, when he became of age, refused to be called the son of Pharaoh's daughter, choosing rather to suffer affliction with the people of God than to enjoy the passing pleasures of sin.*" He is writing about Moses, although raised as part of Pharaoh's family, refusing to indulge in the immoral, but pleasurable, lifestyle of the Egyptians. Moses instead joined with his ancestral people and denied himself the comfort and leisure that lifestyle afforded. Notice it says that the pleasure is passing. Sin is absolutely fun for a while, but there is always a price to be paid. James 1:14-15 reads, "*But each one is tempted when he is drawn away by his own desires and enticed. Then when desire has conceived, it gives birth to sin; and sin, when it is full-grown, brings forth death.*" This is not talking solely about physical death, but there are certainly a lot of sins that lead to literal death. Death is found as the end result of any sin, whether it be death of relationships, death of prosperity, or death of hope.

We have become a generation that thinks little about the consequences of our actions, but the consequences are still there. As wonderful as it would be, our desires that don't line up with God's word don't disappear the moment we give our lives to Jesus. It is a battle every day to deny our flesh. In Luke chapter 9 and verse 23 Jesus made this battle known. It reads, "*Then He said to them all, 'If anyone desires to come after Me, let him deny himself, and take up his cross daily, and follow me.*" Denying ourselves isn't fun. Our human nature wants what we want and wants it now. Jesus is telling us that it is a daily battle to tell our sinful nature "no." In Galatians 5:24, Paul writes, "*Not those who belong to Christ Jesus have crucified the flesh with its passions and desires.*" Crucifixion is an ugly word that infers pain and suffering and there is very little in this world that hurts more than denying yourself. Luckily, we are not forced to deal with this battle on our own. We saw earlier that Paul had gone down this road before and realized that he could not discipline himself enough to avoid sinning. He was transparent with his own battles and failures saying that he still ended up doing the wrong things. In our own strength, we don't have the discipline to resist our wrong desires.

Does that sound bleak? Well, I have good news! God promised that we wouldn't have to do it on our own. In his first letter to the Corinthians, Paul writes in chapter 10 and verses 12-13, "*Therefore let him who thinks he stands take heed lest he fall. No temptation has overtaken you except such as is common to man; but God is faithful, who will not allow you to be tempted beyond what you are able, but with the temptation will also make the way of escape, that you may be able to bear it.*" Temptation isn't a sin, but giving in to it is. Even Jesus was tempted by Satan in the wilderness, and He gave us the example of how to combat any temptation. When Jesus was tempted, He doggedly started off with the same three words: *It is written.* Jesus used the word of God to battle those temptations and we need to do the same. Back in chapter two, we learned that the Bible is a weapon and its primary use is to battle the enemies of our soul. If the Son of God needed a weapon to battle the enemy, how much more do we need it? Whether it is Satan or our sinful nature, the word of God will bring all things into submission.

After giving my life to God and accepting Jesus as my Lord, I was transformed and made a new creature. However, some of my less savory habits wouldn't go away so easily. At the time when I started writing this book, I was still a pretty heavy smoker. I went to church, served on the worship team, and lived a fairly exemplary Christian life, but I liked my cigars...A LOT. Let me be clear that this is my testimony, not a guide for what you should or shouldn't do. It wasn't a healthy habit by any stretch, but neither is overeating or gossiping. I'm not here to debate what is wrong and what isn't. My smoking really didn't bother me at first. However, after a few years, I felt like it was something that was affecting my ability to be a witness to people in my life. I didn't want to quit, but I felt like God was asking me to reevaluate my habits.

After a time in prayer, I felt like God was directing me to start using His word as weapon in this battle. I Corinthians 6:12 reads, "*All things are lawful for me, but all things are not helpful. All things are lawful for me, but I will not be brought under the power of any.*" I would read this verse and others having to do with my body being the temple of the Lord. I also started using my faith and "speaking things that be not as though they are" (Romans 4:17). Every time I would light up a cigar I would thank God for setting me free from this habit. This went on for many months with no perceptible change in my habits.

In another time of prayer some months later, I was praying about another situation entirely, and I felt like God was telling me to give Him a portion of each day with no cigars. I began dedicating four hours each day to God and not smoking during that time. This also went on for a few months. Sometimes I would smoke even more during the rest of the day, but I was faithful with those four hours daily. Having a desire is great, and using your faith is a must, but obedience is where the rubber meets the road with God. I was obedient with what He asked me, even if I didn't understand all of it.

It was some time later in a Wednesday evening service at church that I received the final piece of the puzzle. The worship team was rocking out on stage and I was enjoying a time of worship and praise when I sensed God telling me something. No, once again it wasn't an audible voice, but it was crystal clear in my spirit. He said that the time had come and that I wasn't to smoke anymore. I immediately started praying in earnest about this issue. I told God that I was willing, but that I would need Him to give me strength. Loud and clear He said "NO." I was shocked! I sat down and pouted for a minute before asking Him why. The answer I received, as I sat there, was incredibly simple but so profound that it shook me to my roots. God, speaking to me, the way He'll speak to anyone that is listening, said, "I will not give you strength, but I will *be* your strength if you'll stay out of My way. I don't want you to receive one shred of credit for this. If you'll trust Me and give Me the glory for it, I will make this far easier than you could have ever imagined."

I have heard many stories and testimonials of smoking cessation that include shakes, vomiting, headaches, panic attacks, and irritability for at least a few weeks. There is usually significant weight gain as well. All of these expected side effects were what had kept me from giving up smoking for many years. I enjoyed smoking and I did not want to go through the suffering that I thought had to accompany quitting. However, I had been obeying without question for this long, so I wasn't going to stop now. I experienced withdrawal symptoms for approximately two days and they were so mild that I hardly noticed them. People in my life were amazed at how easily I gave it up, and they would try to compliment my discipline and fortitude, but I wasn't having any of that! God deserved 100% of the glory for setting me free from that habit, and I did not hesitate to give it to Him.

Now this was a personal experience, not a guideline for how God does things. God may lead you on an entirely different journey with battles in your life, but this was the journey He led me on. I didn't lose the desire to quit smoking the day I gave my life to Christ, but God was working on me. The process that God led me through was the most important part of my story. He was testing my obedience and willingness to be who He called me to be. I had to be willing to do the little things that didn't always make sense to me. This proved my trust in God and my sensitivity to His voice. While the physical addiction was gone within a few days, in the months that followed, there were times that the temptation to smoke was fairly strong, but God has been my strength. I cannot say I have been flawless in this, but with God's help, I am always able to get back up and keep going.

How can a God that is all-loving and all-good send people to Hell?

This is another question that keeps many people away from Christianity. Many believers simply can't articulate a good answer for this question, and their failure to do so creates frustration for them and fosters unbelief for the one asking. This question is also a favorite for those who delight in trying to make Christians look simple and ignorant. There are a vast number of people that have no agenda other than making Christians look foolish. The answer to this question is not nearly as complicated as you might think. I have listened to experts in Christian apologetics give hour long dissertations on this subject, and while I'm sure that their answers are precise, I will give a much simpler answer that cuts right to the heart of the matter: He doesn't.

Do not misunderstand me; Hell is just as real as Heaven. The New Testament alone references Hell more than 150 times. Of course, the good news of the gospel is that Jesus paid the price for our sin so that we don't have to spend eternity in Hell. As we've discussed in earlier chapters, there is no sin too large or too evil to be cleansed by the blood of Jesus. He did all the work so that we can avoid the judgment that we deserve and spend our eternity with God in Heaven. In fact, in II Peter 3:9, Peter writes, "*The Lord is not slack concerning His promise, as some count slackness, but is longsuffering toward us, not willing that any should perish but that all should come to repentance.*" That's pretty specific in regard to how God feels about it. He desires everyone to repent and accept Him. However, if we refuse God's grace and do not seek His forgiveness, then we are forced to deal with the consequences of our actions. God isn't going to make you repent. He is all-powerful, but He wants us to choose Jesus for ourselves, and He won't force Himself on us.

The idea of an all-knowing, ever-present, and all-powerful sovereign God co-existing with the idea of man having free will is not an easy concept to fathom. There are many believers that think that free will is just an illusion. They believe that everything is preordained and since God knows the beginning from the end, our choices in life were already determined and therefore not choices at all. That line of thought is pretty tempting, as it would remove all pressure to live up to any kind of Godly standard. We would simply exist and then go on to whatever afterlife has been predetermined for us. As stress-free as this kind of life sounds, there are simply too many scriptures that contradict this whole idea. Joshua 24:15 reads, *"And if it seems evil to you to serve the Lord, choose for yourselves this day whom you will serve, whether the gods which you fathers served that were on the other side of the River, or the gods of the Amorites, in whose land you dwell. But for me and my house, we will serve the Lord."* Joshua is letting the Israelites know that the choice of who they would serve is theirs to make.

God Himself gives the children of Israel a similar choice in Deuteronomy 30:19. God says, *"I call heaven and earth as witnesses today against you, that I have set before you life and death, blessing and cursing; therefore choose life, that both you and your descendants may live."* If we truly have no free will, then why would God ask us to choose? He wouldn't.

We cannot leave up to God things that He has left up to us. It has been this way from the very beginning. Genesis 2:16-17 says, "*And the Lord God commanded the man, saying, 'Of every tree of the garden you may freely eat; but of the tree of the knowledge of good and evil you shall not eat, for in the day that you eat of it you shall surely die.*'" Here we see God giving Adam the choice and spelling out the consequences of making the wrong choice. I would say that's proof enough that God does indeed give us a free will. Our salvation itself depends on our choice to accept Jesus. In Revelation 3:20 God is speaking through John and says, "*Behold, I stand at the door and knock. If anyone hears My voice and opens the door, I will come in to him and dine with him, and he with Me.*"

We have some choices to make, and those choices will shape not only our lives, but also our eternal destination. Therefore, if we choose not to accept Jesus and His forgiveness, we are choosing separation from God. No matter what the movies and books may portray, Hell isn't for evil people; it is for people who won't accept Jesus. As we saw earlier, God desires that everyone would be saved from this fate, but He won't decide for us. We have to believe that Jesus died for our sins and that He rose again three days later. We must believe in our hearts and confess with our mouths that Jesus is Lord (Romans 9:9-10). We must choose to live a life that lines up with God's

Word. God does not send anyone to Hell. We make the choice for those decision ourselves!

Why doesn't God answer my prayers?

Ah, here is another one that we all ask at some point during our life. Why doesn't God answer my prayers? This question is usually accompanied by other favorites like 'Is He listening?' 'Does He even care?' and 'How does my dog understand a lot of my English words but I can't speak a lick of dog?' (Okay, that last one may not go with the rest, but it still keeps me up at night sometimes. I mean who is really the smart one here...) Making requests from God is a normal part of prayer. When giving us the model for prayer in Matthew chapter 6 and verse 11, Jesus says, "*Give us this day our daily bread.*" Even in our Master's perfect prayer, he asked God for provision and the meeting of needs. So why would God, ever, NOT answer our prayers?

The answer that encompasses most instances of unanswered prayer is that our faith is not working effectively. Now this can manifest itself in several ways, but one of the main ones is simply asking for wrong things. When I say wrong, I do not necessarily mean sinful. Sometimes the things we pray for aren't precisely corrupt, they are just not what God wants for us. Then again, other times we are trying to satisfy our flesh with things we shouldn't even desire. James 4:3 reads, "*You ask and do not receive, because you ask amiss, that you may spend it on your pleasures.*" However, even if we have the best intentions, God may deny our petition because we don't understand what God is trying to work out in our lives. We always need to remember the first rule of faith. Faith is only effective where the will of God is known. We can't believe for something that is contrary to the will of God and expect to see the power of mountain-moving faith. That kind of power responds to faith when that faith is agreeing with God's Word. First John 5:14-15 says, "*Now this is the confidence that we have in Him, that if we ask anything according to His will, He hears us. And if we know that He hears us, whatever we ask, we know that we have the petitions that we have asked of Him.*" That's encouraging, but we can't leave out the "according to His will." That's the element that unleashes the true power of faith!

Something else that will put a hard stop to your prayers is doubt or unbelief. This may seem obvious, but I am constantly amazed at how many Christians will pray for a healing, provision, or salvation for family members and don't believe their prayers will do any good. Five minutes after praying that Uncle Bob would give his life to the Lord, they start talking about crazy Uncle Bob. How he will probably ruin Christmas dinner again this year with his racist and off-color jokes. That guy is a hot mess and there isn't much hope for him. Well congratulations, you have just undermined your own prayers! We discussed "speaking life" in the last chapter, and it applies to crazy Uncle Bob as much as it does to receiving your healing. What is coming out of your mouth should NEVER contradict what God's Word says. Doubt is certainly part of our human nature, but it is a part of us that needs to be conquered. James 1:6-8 reads, "*But let him ask in faith, with no doubting, for he who doubts is like a wave of the sea driven and tossed by the wind. For let not that man suppose that he will receive anything from the Lord; he is a double-minded man, unstable in all his ways.*" That's some fairly straight talk. This scripture says that you shouldn't expect to receive anything from God if you doubt what you're asking.

The only person to ever have perfect faith throughout His life is Jesus Christ, so don't be too discouraged if your faith isn't perfect. We aren't always going to be "Mr. Confidence" when bringing our needs to God, but we are expected to use what faith we do have. There is a story in the Gospel of Mark that exemplifies this type of faith. A father of a young boy brought his son to Jesus for a healing. This boy was possessed by a demon that caused the boy to convulse uncontrollably. Mark 9:23-24 reads, "*Jesus said to him, 'If you can believe, all things are possible to him who believes.' Immediately the father of the child cried out and said with tears, 'Lord, I believe; help my unbelief!*'" This father was not calm, cool and collected. He cried out with tears and was trying, with everything he possessed, to have faith in Jesus. This man may not have been a giant of faith, but he was using what he had and even asked God to help him with the doubts he still had. I will be the first to admit that I have asked God many times to help me with my unbelief. God meets you where you are and doesn't make you come up to His level. That is some good news indeed!

There is one more major prayer blocker and this one is a bitter pill to swallow. Unforgiveness and strife will render your prayers just as ineffective as a lack of faith will. Jesus, when delivering the Sermon on the Mount, went into great detail about unforgiveness. Matthew 5:23-24 quotes Jesus saying, " *'Therefore if you bring you gift to the altar, and there remember that your brother has something against you, leave your gift there before the altar, and go your way. First be reconciled to your brother, and then come and offer your gift.* '" Jesus was and is a proponent of forgiveness and reconciliation. He implies that to let bitterness or strife creep into your life and relationships will devalue your prayers. Jesus even gives a stronger admonition in the next chapter. Matthew 6:14-15 reads, "*For if you forgive men their trespasses, your heavenly Father will also forgive you. But if you do*

not forgive men their trespasses, neither will your Father forgive your
trespasses."

For those of us who are married, the Apostle Peter presents an
extremely specific piece of counsel. The third chapter of I Peter is dealing
with marriage and proper conduct for husbands and wives. First Peter 3:7
says, "*Husbands, likewise, dwell with them with understanding, giving honor*
to the wife, as to the weaker vessel, and as being heirs together of the grace of
life, that your payers may not be hindered." Naturally we all know that we
should be kind to our spouses, but this gives a new layer to marital spats! Our
communication with our Heavenly Father can actually be stifled by our
marriage relationship. What may seem like a perfectly practical "cold
shoulder" for leaving the garage door open, can result in unanswered prayers.
Just something to think about ladies. (**cough** guys too, I guess)

It is God's good pleasure to answer authentic, heart-felt, earnest
prayers by His children. He isn't looking for reasons to deny us those things
we ask. He is a good Father! Psalms 34:8 reads, "*Oh, taste and see that the*
Lord is good; blessed is the man who trusts in Him." One of my favorite
scriptures about the goodness of God and His desire for us is found in
Matthew 7:9-11. It reads, "*Or what man is there among you who, if his son*

asks for bread, will give him a stone? Or if he asks for a fish, will he give him

a serpent? If you then, being evil, know how to give good gifts to your

children, how much more will your Father who is in heaven give good things

to those who ask Him!" His plans and desires for us are always so much

bigger and better than we can imagine. Trust in Him!

Chapter 6

Finish your Race!

Is it a sprint or a marathon?

As discussed in chapter two, I don't run. Ever. So naturally, the common comparison of a life of Christianity and a race has always slightly irritated me. However, it is not only apropos symbology, but it is the symbology used in the Bible. The author of Hebrews, along with the Apostle Paul, used running a race as a metaphor for living life under Christ. Why? The similarities are striking when you dive into the attributes of each. Both require endurance, both have rewards, both require learning and training, and both involve much preparation. The unique characteristic of this comparison however, is that our Christian life is both a sprint and a marathon.

In a purely physical sense, our lives are like a marathon. Because this life is all we know, the race can seem long and drawn out. The biblical representations of our lives as a race seem to back up the marathon analogy. The author of Hebrews writes in chapter 12 and verse 1, "*Therefore we also, since we are surrounded by so great a cloud of witnesses, let us lay aside every weight, and the sin which so easily ensnares us, and let us run with endurance the race that is set before us.*" It is called an endurance race; that certainly sounds like a marathon. Paul talks about running his course, finishing his race, and obtaining his prize. God knows that we were created human and cannot truly fathom the concept of eternity. That is why He used this type of long-distance imagery in His word. God is nothing if not relatable to our limitations.

In an eternal sense however, our lives on this earth are much like a 40 yard dash. This life is the shortest thing in which we will ever be involved. Our finite minds cannot grasp the concept of eternity. We know that our existence doesn't end when we die, but we still have a hard time wrapping our minds around "forever." However, just because we can't properly imagine eternity does not eliminate its existence. In his second letter, Peter wrote in chapter 3 and verse 8, "*But, beloved, do not forget this one thing, that with the Lord one day is as a thousand years, and a thousand years as one day.*" That gives us a glimpse of how miniscule our lifespan is to an eternal God, and we're destined to share that eternity! How we spend that eternity is a direct reflection of what we accomplish in our lives here on Earth. God has given us a purpose and all of the tools we need to accomplish that purpose through His Son Jesus. Because we don't know anything other than this life, it seems to drag along sometimes; but rest assured, it will be over before we know it. In

James 4:14, he writes, "*Whereas you do not know what will happen tomorrow. For what is your life? It is even a vapor that appears for a little time and then vanishes away.*" The real theme that James is trying to impress upon us is: time is slipping by faster than you know, so make your time count!

Peter Piper picked a peck of passionate, purposeful, planned preparation

Running a 5K is no spur of the moment decision. No one just hops out of bed one morning and decides to compete in the Boston Marathon on the morning of the event. You can't expect to sit on the couch eating chips and watching Netflix for months at a time and then lace up some sneakers one day and be a successful competitor in an ironman triathlon. It just doesn't work like that. The same is true with our Christian life. There are some key elements that are going to be involved in becoming triumphant in this life. This race requires forethought, focus, groundwork, and training. Let's discuss the ingredients of running a successful race.

Passion. Passion is what gets us off the sidelines in the first place. Passion changes us from a spectator to a competitor. If there is no desire to live for Jesus and make Him Lord of our lives, then we won't even make it into the arena. Passion is what motivated me to write this book. There were a lot of areas of Christianity that I wished someone would have explained when

I first gave my life to God. I have a passion for helping untrained Christians navigate the highs and lows of their new life. Passion wasn't the only precept I needed to write, but it had to start there.

Next to Jesus Himself, the greatest example of true passion in the Bible is David. In the Old Testament, King David is called a man after God's own heart. He certainly wasn't perfect, but he had a desire to please God. As king of Israel, David shows unparalleled passion for God and His things. The Psalms are full of David's heartfelt prayers and songs to God. He desperately desired to build a tabernacle in which the Ark of the Covenant and the Glory of God could reside. Psalms 69:9 reads, "*Because zeal for Your house has eaten me up, and the reproaches for those who reproach You have fallen on me*." So great was his passion to build a temple for the Lord that he endured ridicule and scorn from family and enemies alike.

David makes all of the preparations necessary to begin construction but then receives a visit from Nathan, the prophet. He was forbidden by God, as explained by the prophet, to build the temple. However, because of his passion, he sets his son Solomon up for success for the building of the temple. In I Chronicles 22:14-16, David tells his son, "*Indeed I have taken much trouble to prepare for the house of the Lord one hundred thousand talents of gold and one million talents of silver, and bronze and iron beyond measure, for it is so abundant. I have prepared timber and stone also, and you may add to them. Moreover there are workmen with you in abundance: woodsmen and stonecutters, and all types of skillful men for every kind of work. Of gold and silver and bronze and iron there is no limit. Arise and begin working, and the Lord be with you."* This is passion at work!

As we mature in God and if we are sensitive to His voice, we will discover passions of our own. These passions will be the foundation of discovering what God has in store for us. My passion for teaching and helping new Christian converts became evident in my spirit as I became more willing to let Jesus become not just my Savior but my Lord. As I gave Him control, He showed me the channel in which I could best put my passion to use. Naturally, I had to overcome a myriad of fears and feelings of inadequacy when launching out on this endeavor. I am not a pastor, an evangelist, or even on staff at my church. I felt highly unqualified to write a book considering my lack of credentials, degrees, and experiences. However as I came to learn firsthand, with God's calling comes God's equipping. He isn't going to ask you to do anything without giving you the ability to do it with excellence. I almost feel like a plagiarist because God has written most of this book without any input from me! Even so, there is no greater satisfaction than letting your passion come to life with God's blessings and provision.

Purpose. As we looked at David's example, we saw his passion clearly displayed; but we also saw a direction and blueprint for that passion in the form of purpose. His passion was great, but he had intentions for that passion. He had a plan and a purpose to put his passion into action. The Ark of the Covenant was the most holy object belonging to the children of Israel. It was the resting place of the physical manifestation of the glory of God. The Ark had been captured by the Philistines and remained in their possession for seven months. Every city in which the Ark was moved, experienced plague. After being returned to the Israelites, the Ark stayed in the home of Abinadab for 20 years. Thirteen years into the Ark's stay at Abinadab's, David was crowned king. He had purposed in his heart to bring the Ark back to Jerusalem but His passion was to experience the glory of God.

After discovering a desire in myself to help Christians with discipleship after their initial salvation, I needed a purpose to complement my passion. I became involved in teaching the membership classes for my church, but God soon led me to go further than I ever imagined. I started having dreams of writing a book. I didn't really take it seriously at first. I felt like I was vastly unqualified for this kind of major endeavor. But the more I prayed and sought out God's will for my life, I realized that this purpose would follow me around until I either refused to do it, or got busy. In the early days, it was a dead heat between which one I was going to do! Eventually, after tiring of running from God's calling, I gave in. I purposed in my heart to be obedient to Him and give it a go.

Planning. King David had the passion to experience the Glory of the Lord, and he had purposed to bring the Ark of the Covenant to Jerusalem. However, he initially skipped the next step in the process; planning. The Mosaic Law was extremely specific when it came to the Ark, how it was to be handled, and how it was to be moved. David did not consult God or the Law about moving the Ark; he simply tried to do it his own way. The Ark, according to Law, was only to be moved by members of the tribe of Levites and it was to be carried by hand. Instead, David had the Levites put the Ark on a cart pulled by oxen. One of the oxen stumbled and the Ark started to shift. Uzzah, one of the Levites, put his hand out to steady the Ark and was struck down by God. David was horrified and greatly afraid because he had caused this tragedy with his lack of planning and preparation. The Ark was moved into a nearby house and stayed there for three months until David could adequately plan the journey. After consulting the Law and doing things God's way, the Ark was finally moved into Jerusalem.

Once I had finally wrapped my head around the idea that God actually wanted me to write a book, I made several attempts to begin. The first chapter was written and re-written dozens of times. The entire first attempt was scattered, confused, unfocused, and generally a train wreck. I almost gave up the whole idea. I had put little to no preparation in my passionate purposeful endeavor. Jesus tells a parable in Luke chapter 14 and verses 28 through 30 that illustrates this concept perfectly. He says, "*For which of you, intending to build a tower, does not sit down first and count the cost, whether he has enough to finish it – lest, after he has laid the foundation, and is not able to finish, all who see it begin to mock him, saying, 'This man began to build and was not able to finish.'*" A passion is great, and purpose will motivate you to move, but having a plan and being prepared is essential to completing anything for the kingdom of God.

Eventually I spent some time in prayer and was led to create an outline for the book. That one little step gave me the boost I needed to successfully start what has become The Journey. Almost any writer, fiction or non-fiction, will tell you that an outline is helpful if not necessary, but I wanted to do things my way. I learned a lesson that day, not only to listen to God, but to use some practical wisdom and common sense as well! God never skips the details. He dedicated whole chapters in the Old Testament to exact specifications for the building of His temple. He gave instructions for every square inch of His holy dwelling place. If God is the one in the driver's seat of your life, then He will give you the details necessary to make your calling a success!

Focus. Yes, I know it wasn't in the tongue twister sub-heading, but it doesn't start with a 'P' so I couldn't justify putting it in. Focus is the concept that will carry us when all of the other ones have faded. We can certainly lose our passion (or at least the intensity of that passion) when the road gets rocky. Our purpose can wane when dealing with a spiritually dry season (and you will have those occasionally.) Even the best laid plans can backfire quickly (especially if your passion and purpose are weakened.) However, focus can be the method that will push you through to success. The Apostle Paul writes about this type of focus in I Corinthians chapter 9 and verse 24. Continuing with the race analogy he writes, "*Do you not know that those who run in a race all run, but one receives the prize? Run in such a way that you may obtain it.*" Keeping our eye on the prize and focusing on the end-game will result in triumph, even when we grow tired. Paul addresses this specifically in Galatians 6:9 which reads, "*And let us not grow weary while doing good, for in due season we shall reap if we do not lose heart.*"

King David showed a grim determination to get the Ark of the Covenant to Jerusalem no matter what the cost. It would have been easy to forget the whole endeavor after the improper moving had cost a man his life. David felt keenly responsible for that death and was angered greatly by it, but he didn't give up. Second Samuel 6:9 says, "*David was afraid of the Lord that day; and he said, 'How can the ark of the Lord come to me?'*" He felt defeated in that moment, but his determination and focus led him to plan it out the proper way and move the Ark to Jerusalem. His joy was so great upon entering the city with the Ark that he danced before the Lord with all his might.

To my embarrassment, there was about a four year hiatus between chapter three and chapter four of this book. There have been many parts of chapters four through six that have been written about experiences during those four years, but that is no excuse for the delay. I claimed "writer's block" to those who knew I had been writing a book, but that was also no excuse. To put it simply, I lost my focus. I could no longer see the end result. I still had a desire to help people and my outline was still viable, but my focus was gone. The ups and downs of this life stole my focus; and I let it. Time and time again, God put people in my path to remind me about the task assigned to me, but by then, I was overwhelmed. I had begun to see this book as a fantasy that would never be realized. Thankfully, God never gives up on us. Eventually, I got tired of running from this calling and I buckled down and started writing again. With a renewed focus, the last few chapters have flown by as quickly as the first few did. Now as I am approaching the end of the book, I feel a joy that is simply indescribable. Passion, purpose, planning and focus will allow you to not only finish the race, but finish it with unspeakable joy!

Patience: the universally despised virtue

NO! You get back here! Don't you dare skip this section! I know, I know…nobody wants to talk about patience. The old saying of "patience is a virtue" is true, but that doesn't make it anymore endearing. I did a fairly exhaustive study on patience a few years ago and discovered that it isn't nearly as vile a word as most people think. In fact, I had told some of my church friends that I was actively praying that God would help teach me patience and they all looked at me like I had grown another head. To those friends of mine, and to most Christians that I have talked to, praying for patience is like praying for trouble. I used to think about it the same way.

When talking to believers about patience, they always seem to want to bring up Jacob. "Poor old Jacob had to work for his father-in-law for fourteen years to get his promised bride. God was teaching him patience." What most people forget is that Jacob's name means "deceiver." God wasn't teaching Jacob patience, he was teaching him character! Had Jacob caught on a little earlier, God would have allowed him to get his wife sooner. When the Bible says that we reap what we sow, this is a pretty good example. Jacob manipulated to get his brother's birthright and then lied to his father to get the blessing meant for Esau. He wasn't the picture of integrity. God knew that Jacob was destined to be a leader and was forced to break him of this deceitful nature. The sooner that we can become men and women of integrity, the easier time God will have in transforming us into what He desires.

Nonetheless, most Christians think that it's crazy to pray for patience. They think if you pray for patience, your patience will be tested constantly. This simply isn't true. Patience is a fruit of the Spirit. The very nature of fruit is that there is a waiting period while it grows and ripens. The other fruits of the Spirit aren't treated as unfairly. We wouldn't think twice to pray for peace, love or gentleness, but heaven forbid we should pray for patience. Far too many Christians when considering patience have an image of God holding what we want just out of our reach...almost teasing us. This is such an unfair and flat out false image of our loving Father. Jeremiah 29:11 says, "*For I know the thoughts that I think toward you, says the Lord, thoughts of peace and not of evil, to give you a future and a hope.*" Does this sound like a God that likes to hold good things out of reach of His kids? I don't think so. So why do we have to wait so often?

One reason to develop patience is to offset our stupidity. I know that sounds a little harsh, but as I look back on a lifetime of prayers, I see that many of my prayers were foolish. Actually, ignorant would be a better word. I didn't see the big picture when I was praying. Aren't you glad we have a heavenly Father that isn't constrained by time and has already been in our tomorrow? He knows exactly what we need, and it is always easier and more satisfying than what we could imagine. I remember being single and praying for a house. I looked at dozens, but was never financially able to move. I didn't know why God wasn't helping me. I was using my faith the best I knew how, and I never stopped believing, no matter how frustrated I became. However, three years later after getting married and becoming a family of six, I understood why God didn't deliver when I asked. Brandi and I bought the first house we looked at! It was exactly what we needed and I had to go back and thank God for making me wait. His way is always more satisfying than ours.

We discussed asking God for things contrary to His will back in the FAQ section and this is a common reason for awaiting period. It gives us time to get our wishes and desires in line with God's will. Sometimes if you push hard enough, God will let you have your way. This has happened to me and IT WAS AWFUL! I got exactly what I had been praying for, and it turned into an unmitigated disaster. I try to never push God to do it my way anymore. The Israelites did this with God after getting to the Promised Land. They were presided over by judges that were appointed by God. However, they wanted a king like all of the other nations. They pressed and pressed until God relented and anointed a king over Israel. That was the beginning of centuries of war and bloodshed. God will sometimes let you have your way, if only to show you that His way would have been so much better!

The foremost reason to develop patience is obedience to God's word. Ephesians 4:1-2 reads, "*I, therefore, the prisoner of the Lord, beseech you to walk worthy of the calling with which you were called, with all lowliness and gentleness, with longsuffering, bearing with one another in love.*" Longsuffering is another word for patience and describes how we are to be with one another.

God's word talks about being patient with one another several times. Romans 12:10-12 says, *"Be kindly affectionate to one another with brotherly love, in honor giving preference to one another; not lagging in diligence, fervent in spirit, serving the Lord; rejoicing in hope, patient in tribulation, continuing steadfastly in prayer."* Of course we are also to develop patience with our spiritual growth and maturation. James writes in his letter in chapter 5 verse 8, *"You also be patient. Establish your hearts, for the coming of the Lord is at hand."* Chapter 1 and verses 2-4 of the same book read, *"My brethren, count it all joy when you fall into various trials, knowing that the testing of your faith produces patience. But let patience have its perfect work, that you may be perfect and complete, lacking nothing."* These scriptures are merely a sample. There are over 50 scriptures mentioning patience in the Bible. If God considers it that important, we should too!

Back in chapter three we talked about how important and essential faith is to our growth in Christ. We learned that without faith it is impossible to please God. However, we only have as much faith as we have patience. That's a pretty bold statement, but scripture indicates that this is truth.

Hebrews 10:35-36 reads, "*Therefore do not cast away your confidence, which has great reward. For you have need of endurance, so that after you have done the will of God, you may receive the promise.*" Faith that doesn't endure isn't faith at all. When you are willing to hold on until you see God's promises become reality, then you are showing true patience, therefore showing true faith! The author of Hebrews mentions this again in chapter 6 and verses 11-12. He says, "*And we desire that each one of you show the same diligence to the full assurance of hope until the end, that you do not become sluggish, but imitate those who through faith and patience inherit the promise.*"

This life may be the shortest thing we ever do, but there are times when it is going to drag on worse than a foreign subtitled documentary. Patience is going to be a necessary and vital tool at our disposal. Without patience, we will quickly grow frustrated and tired of waiting. Remember, this race is a marathon. Hebrews 12:1 sums it up pretty well. "*Therefore we also, since we are surrounded by so great a cloud of witnesses, let us lay aside every weight, and the sin which so easily ensnares us, and let us run with endurance the race that is set before us.*" Whether we know it or not, people are watching us. Let us show the world how to run this race with endurance!

The greatest trick the devil ever pulled

As I began to write this section, God began dealing with me about Satan (Beelzebub, Lucifer, the Devil, etc.) He spoke to my spirit and told me that most of His children deal with the enemy of our souls in one of two ways. Either they don't really think that Satan exists, or they believe he is pure evil **AND** the equal of God. Satan loves to encourage either of these viewpoints. He has a free reign in our life if we don't believe he even exists. The Bible says to resist the Devil and he will flee from us; but why would we resist someone in whom we don't believe. On the other hand, there are people who see the Devil under every rock. They give him credit for every negative thing in their lives. If their car breaks down, it was the Devil (even though they haven't changed the oil in 8000 miles). If they sprain their ankle, the Devil is trying to keep them down (even though they decided to play tackle football with kids 20 years younger than them). If they oversleep on Sunday and miss church, it's the Devil waging war on them (even though they stayed up until 4 am marathoning through an entire season of Firefly on Netflix). Our own bad decisions and life choices have as much to do with negative consequences in our life as the enemy most of the time. However, this is not to say that Satan doesn't go after the church. He does indeed. And the more effective you are as a Christian, the more of a threat you are to the Devil.

Satan is real and he is crafty. He has been around a long time and is very good at what he does. He has been playing mind games with humanity since the Garden of Eden. Genesis 3:1 reads, *"Now the serpent was more cunning than any beast of the field which the Lord God had made. And he said to the woman, 'Has God indeed said, 'You shall not eat of every tree of the garden?'"* He has been a plotter and deceiver from the moment he rebelled against God. He began as an angel of light in heaven, but was cast out when he tried to take the place of God. Deceit and vanity are two of his most used tools, but he will stop at nothing to obstruct the spread of the Gospel. This may bring to mind death, mayhem, and destruction, but usually he is much more subtle. The Devil desires nothing more than to keep the church silent and ineffective, but he normally doesn't need earthquakes and terminal illnesses to do that; seeds of doubt, pride, or envy serves him just as well. The battlefield for the enemy will always be the mind. If he can plant these seeds, our fallen nature will usually finish the job for him. Our flesh doesn't need any encouragement to be selfish or prideful. The only requirement to give in to these attitudes is to wake up in the morning. Our heart may be saved, but our human nature isn't. However, the biggest deception that Satan uses in the church is that he is the "ying to God's yang."He wants us to believe that the sides are stacked pretty evenly and somehow the outcome of the war for our soul is a real coin-toss.

A few years ago, I was channel surfing and I came across a baseball game. While I am not a "glued to the TV 162 nights a year" fanatic, I do enjoy an occasional game. This particular game was in the 5th inning and pitted my beloved St. Louis Cardinals against a division rival. The score was tied and it was looking to be an exciting game. It turned out to be a nail-biter. Three lead changes going into the bottom of the ninth with the Cards down by one. I was now emotionally invested in this contest. What was going to happen? Was the opponent's bullpen going to hold up? The Redbirds had a few comebacks in the last week. Was it going to happen again? There are now two men on base and two outs. My stomach is in knots. How is it going to end? Right about then, a friend of mine walks into the room and looks at the television.

"All right! I want to see this again!" he said.

"What are you talking about?" I replied.

"He walks this guy to load the bases and the next guy gets a walk off double. Didn't you watch this last night?" he asked.

It was the previous night's game being replayed. I never even noticed the little replay banner in the top right of the screen. Not only did I feel like an idiot for not noticing the banner, but I felt foolish for being stressed out about it as well. I had let myself get totally worked up over a game that's conclusion was already decided.

Millions of Christians worldwide do the exact same thing with the enemy. We worry. We get stressed. We live in anxiety. And all the while, the Bible that is right under our nose tells us that Satan has already been defeated. When Jesus died on the cross, He took all authority back from the Devil. Satan isn't the equal opposition to God. He would like you to think that, but it just isn't true. Satan is a created being that started out his existence as an angel, but was cast out of heaven. Pride and vanity convinced Lucifer that he should be worshipped too. Isaiah 14:13-15 reads, "*For you have said in your heart: 'I will ascent into heaven, I will exalt my throne above the stars of God; I will also sit on the mount of the congregation on the farthest sides of the north; I will ascend above the heights of the clouds, I will be like the Most High.' Yet you shall be brought down to Sheol, to the lowest depths of the Pit.*" And in Revelation 20:10, John records Satan's final destination as he says, "*The Devil, who deceived them, was cast into the lake of fire and brimstone where the beast and the false prophet are. And they will be tormented day and night forever and ever.*" Does this sound like an entity that is the match of Almighty God? Not hardly! Satan is a created, fallen, and ultimately defeated adversary.

So why am I waiting around until the last chapter to deal with Lucifer? I waited because understanding who and what he is has major implications for running our race. Yes, he is real and will try to mess with us. Yes, he is a master of mind games. Yes, in our own strength and wisdom, we would be easy fodder for Satan. However, we have Jesus Christ living on the inside of us! First John 4:4 reads, "*You are of God, little children, and have overcome them, because He who is in you is greater than he who is in the world.*" Becoming stressed out and upset over the enemy's tactics and actions is just like me getting upset over that baseball game. Reading the Bible, we know exactly how the cards play out. We end up in eternity with our God, and the Devil ends up chained and cast out! The game is already over and we win!

It ain't in how you start

Imagine if you will this scenario. You have just finished college. You have earned your Master's Degree and are ready to attend your first job interview. You felt a little nervous this morning, but now you are confident that you meet all of the criteria for this job posting. You are dressed in your

Sunday best and arrive promptly. As the interviewer walks you into his office, you are calm and ready. You are determined to maintain eye contact and project absolute assurance that you are the right person for the job. After you are both seated, the interview begins.

"So, you feel that you are adequately qualified for this position?" he asks.

"Yes sir, I think my resume speaks for itself," you reply.

"Hmmmm…. Yes, your credentials are impressive, but I would like to discuss the background check we ran."

"Uh… okay. I'm quite certain that I have nothing incriminating in there," I said.

"Yes, well there were a few items that we found disturbing, but I wanted to give you the chance to clear the air and be honest with us."

"I'm sure there must be a mistake here. I have no criminal background at all," you reply rather heatedly. This is not going the way it is supposed to go.

"No, nothing criminal, just some disturbing occurrences and tendencies that might not be the best fit here at our firm," he explains.

"Like what?!" you demand. This interview is definitely coming off the rails.

"Well, it says here that you often spit up your vegetables, or at times even hide them under your mattress."

"WHAT?! I haven't done that since I was two years old!" you nearly shout.

"So you admit that it's true, hmmm. How about this tendency to shoot your cat with a Super Soaker?"

"Again… I was a little kid when I used to do that," you explain. You are becoming thoroughly confused by these accusations.

"Are you still unruly and distracting at nap time?" he asks while checking things off on his clipboard.

"ARE YOU KIDDING ME??!!"

How frustrating would this be? You have spent the last ten years of your life studying diligently and preparing yourself for a rewarding career, but all the interviewer wants to talk about is your early childhood. I guess your kindergarten teacher wasn't joking when she said your disruptiveness would go on your permanent record! Naturally this fictional scenario is absurd, but there is some truth to it as well. The only real difference is that we're usually the ones that are hung up on our own past. Even if we are able to understand and accept God saving and forgiving us from our life before knowing him, we often still punish ourselves for mistakes we make as new Christians. This can become a major hindrance when trying to keep our eye on the prize. Running even a few yards while looking backward can lead to an ugly fall. Imagine what running a marathon while having our heads turned around will do.

The good news is this: how we start isn't nearly as important as how we finish. Just like our natural childhood, our early Christian walk will be rife with mistakes, immaturity, and ignorance. We can't skip years two through seventeen in real life, and we can't skip the growing up process as a believer either. However, just as in our physical maturing, our Christian maturing will produce experiences that are vital to becoming complete. Fortunately, if we are diligent and follow the guidelines set forth in scripture, we have no choice except to become mature believers. Paul writes in Philippians 1:6, "*being confident of this very thing, that He who has begun a good work in you will complete it until the day of Jesus Christ.*" Maturity and completeness is promised and assured as long as we do our part. Loving God, loving people, and keeping God's commandments are the ingredients for a healthy Christian life. Fortunately, how we finish the race is much more important than how we start.

The Apostle Paul started out as a thoroughly disreputable man named Saul. He was a persecutor of Christians everywhere and was even a consenting party to the killing of Stephen, a Christian disciple. Jesus confronted Saul on the road to a city named Damascus. After his conversion, he went on to preach the Gospel all over Europe and he wrote two-thirds of the New Testament. He testified of Jesus Christ before kings and emperors. Do you think he finished well? I'd say so, but I actually want to talk about one of Paul's contemporaries, John Mark.

John Mark, or Mark as he is commonly referred in the New Testament, was the younger cousin of Barnabas. Barnabas was a fellow missionary who accompanied the Apostle Paul on his first famine relief trip to Antioch. During Paul and Barnabas' second missionary journey, they took Barnabas' cousin John Mark as their assistant. The Bible is not overly specific about what happened to Mark during this trip, but he leaves the two apostles in the middle of the journey. Acts 13:13 reads, "*Now when Paul and his party set sail from Paphos, they came to Perga in Pamphylia; and Mark, departing from them, returned to Jerusalem.*" Now you might not think much of such a nondescript departure, but more light is shed on this event when it came time for the next mission trip.

Acts 15:36-40 reads, "*Then after some days Paul said to Barnabas, 'Let us now go back and visit our brethren in every city where we have preached the word of the Lord, and see how they are doing.' Now Barnabas was determined to take with them John called Mark. But Paul insisted that they should not take with them the one who had departed from them in Pamphylia, and had not gone with them to the work. Then the contention became so sharp that they parted from one another. And so Barnabas took Mark and sailed to Cyprus; but Paul chose Silas and departed, being commended by the brethren to the grace of God.*" The Apostle Paul obviously viewed Mark as a deserter. While Barnabas was willing to vouch for his cousin, Paul wanted someone else. This argument split up their team.

Since all biblical narrative of Barnabas ends here, it would be easy to write Mark off as an immature or half-hearted Christian. Paul goes on with his life and ministry. However, near the end of Paul's life when he is imprisoned in Rome, he writes a letter to Timothy. All of his partners in ministry save one have departed from him. He beseeches his protégé, Timothy, to come to him. He writes in 2 Timothy 4:11, "*Only Luke is with me. Get Mark and bring him with you, for he is useful to me for ministry.*" WHAT? Is this the same Mark that Paul was so adamant to leave behind? It is! While the Bible may not tell us what happened, we can make a pretty good assumption that Mark grew up. Sure, when he was younger he made mistakes, but he ended up proving his value and worth to the greatest Apostle in the New Testament!

What a story of redemption this is. He may have not started off strong, but Mark ended well. This example should be such an encouragement to all of us. We all have to go through the "baby Christian" stage. We can't skip it. We will learn valuable lessons, we will end up with scrapes on our knees, but we will grow. Our beginning, as important as those first few steps are, is not indicative of how we will finish. Let us determine in our hearts, in our minds, and in our spirits that we will finish our race better than we began. The Apostle Paul puts into words what each of us should strive for in 2 Timothy 4:7-8. He says, "*I have fought the good fight, I have finished the race, I have kept the faith. Finally, there is laid up for me the crown of righteousness, which the Lord, the righteous Judge, will give me on that Day, and not to me only but also to all who have loved His appearing.*"

Whether you are a new Christian trying to learn the ropes of your new life, or a seasoned mature believer that just needs refreshing, I hope this book has helped you. I know that I have learned so much in writing it. Probably the most important lesson I have learned is humility. Every time I tried to write my own words and feelings, it came out all wrong. With God's calling comes His abilities and I'm so thankful for that. To Him be all of the Glory. God Bless.

Conclusion

Every believer on this planet has a different story to tell. Each person's relationship with Jesus is a personal and extremely subjective experience. I have related many stories of my own journey here in these pages, but those stories are meant as encouragements, not blueprints. Each of you will have your own methods, outlines, and lessons to be learned. Please don't try to dilute your experiences to model after or match mine! While some may see this book as a "How To" guide, it is actually just a collection of experiences and information that I would have found helpful in the early days of my own Christian conversion.

There are times that you will fail. This is not meant to be discouraging, but to impress upon you that life still happens. The great part about it however, is that with God in your life, you have the ability to overcome ANYTHING! Naturally, you can't be an overcomer if there is nothing to overcome. Use the obstacles that life and the enemy throws at you to exercise your faith. Before giving your life to God, you had little to no control over anything, but with Jesus as your master, you will find the list of things that you can alter with your faith is MUCH longer! The more confident you become in God's power and His goodness, the more effective your faith will become. Trust in God and He will show Himself might on your behalf!

I can't help but feel empty now that I'm done writing, but it is a good empty. I feel like I have poured out what God has put in me, and am now ready for fresh revelation, fresh goals, and a new dream. My ultimate goal is always to advance the kingdom of God in whatever way He directs me and I am excited to see what the next chapter holds.

Endnotes

Scripture References by chapter

Chapter 1

I Corinthians 1:18

Acts 26:20

Romans 13:14

Matthew 7:1-2

Acts 13:22

Romans 10:9

Romans 8:6

Chapter 2

Deuteronomy 6:5

I John 4:4

Hebrews 10:25

Hebrews 3:13

Romans 10:17

Psalms 119:105

Acts 17:26-27

I Corinthians 10;13

Genesis 2:18

Ephesians 4:11-12

Hebrews 4:12

John 14:21

Ephesians 6:17	Mark 11:22-24
Isaiah 53:5	Philippians 4:19
I John 4:4	Romans 8:1
Matthew 6:9-13	John 4:23
Acts 7:51	James 4:22
Mark 11:24	Mark 11:25
James 1:13	I Corinthians 10:13
Luke 19:40	Daniel 6:10

Chapter 3

Hebrews 5:12-14	Colossians 1:10
Genesis 1:26	James 1:22-25
Hebrews 11:6	Colossians 3:23
Hebrews 6:10-12	Genesis 2:2
Genesis 2:15	Proverbs 3:6

Romans 8:11	Luke 14:28-30
Proverbs 27:17	Romans 15:14
Galatians 6:1-2	Genesis 8:22
Jeremiah 1:5	II Peter 3:9
Hebrews 11:1	Romans 12:3
John 14:15	Hebrews 5:12-14
Psalms 84:11	II Corinthians 9:8
Acts 13:47	I Corinthians 15:57
II Timothy 2:15	II Peter 3:9
Psalms 103:2-4	I Peter 2:24
Matthew 6:31-32	Philippians 4:19
Psalms 29:11	Galatians 5:1
Isaiah 61:8-9	John 14:15
I Samuel 2:30	Habakkuk 3:17-19

James 1:2-4	Isaiah 1:19
Romans 2:6-8	Philippians 4:19
James 3:3-12	Proverbs 18:21
Mark 11:22-23	Luke 6:45
James 1:26	Ecclesiastes 10:12
Proverbs 11:9	Mark 6:3-6
Job 3:25	Matthew 12:37-37
Proverbs 17:27	Proverbs 13:3
Proverbs 10:19	

Chapter 4

John 9:39-41	Romans 5:13
Romans 6:1	Romans 6:14-16
Galatians 5:13	Galatians 5:24

John 14:15

Matthew 5:48

II Timothy 3:16-17

Psalms 38:17-18

Acts 13:22

Romans 8:1

Genesis 3:8-10

James 5:16

Proverbs 27:17

Hebrews 13:11-12

Matthew 26:28

Hebrews 9:13-14

Hebrews 10:26

Deuteronomy 18:13

Isaiah 43:25

Psalms 40:12

Revelation 12:10

II Corinthians 7:10

Revelation 12:10-11

Proverbs 25:12

Galatians 6:1-2

Ephesians 1:7

I John 1:6

Chapter 5

Luke 13:1-5	John 16:33
Nehemiah 8:10	Romans 5:3-5
John 9:1-3	Romans 7:18-19
Romans 7:24	Hebrews 11:24-25
James 1:14-15	Luke 9:23
Galatians 5:24	ICorinthians 10:12-13
I Corinthians 6:12	Romans 4:17
II Peter 3:9	Joshua 24:15
Deuteronomy 30:19	Genesis 2:16-17
Revelation 3:20	Romans 9:9-10
Matthew 6:11	James 4:3
John 5:14-15	James 1:6-8
Mark 9:23-24	Matthew 5:23-24

Matthew 6:14-15

Psalms 34:8

I Peter 3:7

Matthew 7:9-11

Chapter 6

Hebrews 12:1

James 4:14

I Chronicles 22:14-16

I Corinthians 9:24

II Samuel 6:9

Ephesians 4:1-2

James 5:8

Hebrews 10:35-36

Hebrews 12:1

Isaiah 14:13-15

I John 4:4

II Peter 3:8

Psalms 69:9

Luke 14:28-30

Galatians 6:9

Jeremiah 29:11

Romans 12:10-12

James 1:2-4

Hebrews 6:11-12

Genesis 3:1

Revelation 20:10

Philippians 1:6

Acts 13:13   Acts 15:36-40

II Timothy 4:11   II Timothy 4:7-8

Lightning Source UK Ltd.
Milton Keynes UK
UKHW02f1941070818
326899UK00010B/443/P